# PIVOTAL LEADERS

## 21 PRINCIPLES TO CONTINUALLY THINK BIGGER AND REACH HIGHER IN CHANGING TIMES

Loren Murfield, PhD

*PIVOTAL LEADERS*

© 2024 Loren O. Murfield, Ph.D.

All rights reserved. No part of this book may be used or reproduced in any manner whatsoever without the written permission of the publisher, Murfield International, Inc. Printed in the United States of America. For information, contact Loren O. Murfield at Loren@MurfieldCoaching.com

# DEDICATION

*To those willing to live beyond the comfort and safety of predictability.*

# BOOKS BY DR. MURFIELD

**Business & Professional Development Books**

Pivotal Apathy: Secrets to Letting Go of Things That Don't Matter (2021)

Pivotal Business: 8 Gears to Lead Your Business from a Chevette to a Corvette. (2007, 3rd Ed. 2020)

Pivotal Compassion: 4 Strategic Steps to Unleash the Ultimate Performance, Production, and Profits in Traumatic Times. Lisa & Loren Murfield (2nd Ed. 2018)

Pivotal Conversations with My Future Self: Book 1: Identifying the Prize Inside (2020)

Pivotal Conversations with My Future Self: Book 2: Valuing, Owning, Sharing and Secrets to Becoming a Disruptive Leader (2020)

Pivotal Engagement: 4 Steps to Create an Innovative Culture. Loren & Lisa Murfield. (2019)

Pivoting From Stupid: How to Make S.M.A.R.T. Decisions and Stop Being S.T.U.P.I.D. in Times of Opportunity (2020)

Pivotal Leaders: 21 Principles to Continually Thinking Bigger and Reaching Higher in the Next Normal. (2021)

Pivotal Listening: Building Your Breakthrough Team with Compassion, Strategy and Power. (2020)

Pivotal Living and Working. (2021)

Pivotal Networking: 5 Steps to Build Great Relationships, Increase Sales, and Seize Your Best Opportunities. (2020)

Pivotal Opportunities: Utilizing Your 6 Senses to Sense and Seize Opportunities When You Need Them Most (2nd Ed. 2018)

Pivotal Paradigm Shift: Making Money in Tough Times by Asking One Disruptive Question. (3rd Ed. 2020)

Pivotal Power: How to Leverage the 4 Critical Elements of Cutting-Edge Teams. (2021)

Pivotal Procrastination: (2023) How I ALMOST Made $1 Million: Your Guide to Take the Right Action at the Right Time. (2023)

Pivotal Thinking: 4 Types of Thinking to Create Your Breakthrough. Thinking Bigger to Make Smart Decisions and Avoid Unnecessary Problems. (2020/2024)

Your Pivotal Prize Inside: The Parable of a Little Boy with a Big Idea (2019)

**Legacy Books**

Just One More: How I Ran 6 Marathons in the Year I Turned 68 (2024)

## PIVOTAL LEADERS

Too Tough To Quit 2024: Inspirational Stories from the 2024 Chicago Marathon Back-of-the-Pack Runners (2024)
Too Tough To Quit: 12 Inspirational Stories from the 2023 Chicago Marathon Back of the Pack Runners (2023)
Medal Monday: My Quest to Run 50 Marathons in 50 States in 50 Weeks 5 Years after Being Shot 5 Times. With Aaron Burros. (2022)
Pitchfork to Ph.D.: The Journey from "I AM a Chore Boy Follower" to "I AM a Disruptive Leader. (2021)
10 Minutes of Insanity. Coauthored with Heisman Winner Johnny Rodgers (2016)
Humble Homesteaders: A South Dakota Story of Integrity (2010)

**Spiritual Books**
Turbulent Serenity: Unleash Your Ultimate Spiritual Life (2011)
Heavenly Opportunities: Unleash Your Ultimate Relationship with God (2011)
God's Workmanship: Unleash the Ultimate Spiritual Relationship with Ourselves (2011)
Fellow Travelers: Unleash Your Ultimate Spiritual Relationship with Others (2011)
Resurrection: The Ultimate Opportunity (2011)

**Meditation Books**
Guided Meditations from the National Parks: Introduction (2023)
More Guided Meditations from the National Parks: Part 2 of the Introduction (2025)
Guided Meditations for the National Parks for Business Innovations (2025)
Awe: Guided Meditations from the Grand Canyon National Park (2024)
Experience: Guided Meditations from the Haleakala National Park (2025)
History: Guided Meditations from the Great Smoky Mountains National Park (2024)
Humility: Guided Meditations from Redwoods, Muir Woods, Sequoia, and Kings Canyon National Parks (2025)
Journey: Guided Meditations from the Bryce Canyon Mountains National Park (2024)
Majesty: Guided Meditations from Mt. Rainier National Monument (2024)
Measured: Guided Meditations from Wind Cave National Park (2024)
Mystery: Guided Meditations from the Great Smoky Mountains National Park (2024)
Opportunities: Guided Meditations from Olympic National Park (2024)
Power: Guided Meditations from Mt. St. Helens National Monument (2024)

*PIVOTAL LEADERS*

Protection: Guided Meditations from the Everglades National Park (2024)
Reach Higher: Guided Meditations from Rocky Mountain National Park (2024)
Strength: Guided Meditations from Zion National Park (2024)
Surprise: Guided Meditations from the Badlands National Park (2024)
Ultimate: Guided Meditations from Yosemite National Park (2024)
Vulnerable: Guided Meditations from Glacier National Park (2024)
Unbridled: Guided Meditations from North Cascades National Park
Wonder: Guided Meditations from Yellowstone National Park (2024)

*PIVOTAL LEADERS*

## TABLE OF CONTENTS

INTRODUCTION: THE NEED FOR CONTINUOUS PIVOTING .......... 9
RECOGNIZING A MAJOR DISRUPTION ......................................... 19
MAKING YOUR PIVOTAL CHANGE................................................ 28
21 PRINCIPLES.................................................................................. 36
1. TRACK THE TRENDS – FORECAST THE OPPORTUNITIES...... 38
\2: STAY FOCUSED............................................................................ 55
3: ENGAGE YOUR TEAM................................................................. 64
4: FOSTER AN INNOVATIVE CULTURE ....................................... 77
5: FIND YOUR UNIQUE VALUE ..................................................... 87
6: CHALLENGE YOUR TEAM......................................................... 94
7: COMMUNICATE .......................................................................... 98
8: SHARE YOUR INNOVATIVE VISION ...................................... 114
9: LEVERAGE FEAR ....................................................................... 120
10: LEVERAGE PAIN ...................................................................... 126
11: BE AGGRESSIVE IN YOUR STRATEGY................................ 135
12: FOSTER DISRUPTION ............................................................. 141
13: RETHINK REJECTION & FAILURE ....................................... 145
14: CREATE A CUTTING-EDGE ATTITUDE ............................... 149
15: FOSTER FLEXIBILITY............................................................. 154
16: BREAK THE RULES ................................................................. 160
17: OVERCOME ANY OBSTACLE................................................ 168
18: COLLABORATE ........................................................................ 178
19: BREAK THROUGH ................................................................... 183
20: THINK EVEN BIGGER............................................................. 188
21: MAKE DISRUPTION A HABIT ............................................... 193
YOUR PIVOTAL CHALLENGE....................................................... 197

REFERENCES ............................................................................ 199
PIVOTAL LIVING AND WORKING SERIES .................................. 204
GUIDED BUSINESS MEDITATIONS from the NATIONAL PARKS SERIES .................................................................................... 205
GUIDED MEDITATIONS from the NATIONAL PARKS SERIES ... 206
VIDEO COURSES and SERIES .................................................. 207
NOW AVAILABLE ..................................................................... 208
ABOUT THE AUTHOR ............................................................... 209

# INTRODUCTION: THE NEED FOR CONTINUOUS PIVOTING

The challenge for modern leaders is not simply to pivot through Tough Times but to continually shift to sense and seize the best opportunities. With the world changing radically and rapidly, the modern leader must continually swivel their focus from the past or present to the future. They must keep one foot firmly planted in the present while shifting not just their head, but upper body, to fine tune their focus on the future. Modern leaders cannot be content with a single pivot but rather must become pivotal. The world is changing too much and too fast for change to be a onetime occurrence.

We all enjoy a stable sense of Normal where life is predictable and therefore safe and comfortable. Tough Times, those interruptions to our normal routine, leaves us without at least one of those three elements. When an economic recession begins, like in 2007, we cannot predict how deep it will be or how long it would last. When the Covid pandemic started in 2020, we couldn't predict what life would look like during or after a shutdown. In the same way, our individual Tough Times include the absences of predictability, safety, and comfort when we lose a job, material possessions, or a loved one.

Tough Times shatter our normal lives.

It doesn't matter whether it is a terrorist attack, divorce, or bankruptcy, Tough Times turn our stable and enjoyable lives into rubble. The only choice we have is to choose to create our lives in the next new normal. That requires a difficult pivot.

**Past Pivots**

Looking back, we can see three major events just since 2000 that have radically altered our perspective of the world. The 9-11 terrorist attacks on New York City and Washington, D.C. forever changed the American psyche. Suddenly we had to pivot to see a world where mass transportation could be used to pursue a devastating political agenda. That same agenda was played out in the Boston Marathon bombing. To be go forward, we had to pivot and adapt new safety measures.

The second event was the 2008 recession. We enjoyed the roaring economy. We enjoyed the relaxed regulations, busying houses on stated rather than proven income. But then the bubble burst, sending tremors around the world. We struggled for years to revive the economy.    In the process, many suffered economically. Worse yet, no one could predict when it would return. No wonder there was so little comfort during those Tough Times.

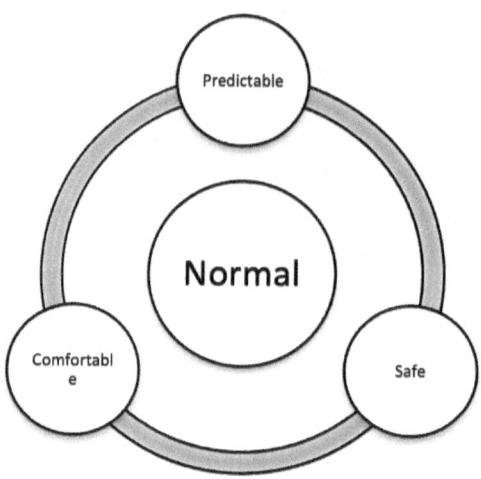

The third major event was the Covid pandemic. This time, threatened by an invisible disease, the world was shut down. There was no escape, nowhere to flee. Every country quarantined and closed their borders. No matter where you were, the virus was a threat.

Notice the financial, physical, and emotional threats to our lives during these Tough Times. Then notice the lingering effects of each. 9-11 left us forever concerned about the safety of mass transportation. The recession left us wondering how long the good times can last. The virus left us wondering how to protect our health from an invisible threat.

Then notice the other Tough Times we are currently facing. Racial unrest has percolated into the streets. Political polarization has created an emotional civil war, separating friends and families. Science is doubted, tradition defied, and culture questioned. Our world is rapidly and awkwardly struggling to pivot into the Next Normal. In the process, we are entering an unpredictable world. That is threatening and uncomfortable for many, if not most.

## PIVOTAL LEADERS

If only we could see what we were pivoting into, but we can't see it. That is partly due to many not willing to look forward. While some are convinced the world needs to change, many others deny any need. Some are arguing it isn't changing far or fast enough and others that we have already gone too far. What we can see is that collectively, the pivot is threatening to tear us apart.

### Balance

To pivot requires several components of balance, as seen in the Warrior yoga position. Leaders are challenged to balance balancing the past with the present, and the present with the future. We must keep one foot securely in the future, while reaching for the best opportunities of the future. Meanwhile, there is increasing pressure to denounce the past, yet we understand what is behind us helps balance what is in front of us. The challenge for leaders is to pivot between the three in a way that creates a balance.

Notice how difficult it is to strike that pose for any length of time unless you have worked diligently to build your core strength. Whether in yoga, business or life, balance is a core issue.

Without that balance, disruption quickly knocks us off our feet. We don't have the strength, in part, because we haven't exercised the pivot. We have sat or walked, maybe even been running without paying attention to our core.

Our lack of balance is revealed easiest after a traumatic disruption. Maybe that is why the process of pivoting may be just as traumatic as the disruption itself. In our research and work on our three compassion books, my wife and I have detailed the struggle of balancing extremes. Leaders struggle to balance praising their teams with a pat on the back or pushing them with a kick in the backside. Middle managers especially struggle to balance the demands of upper management and the needs of front-line workers. Within each of your positions, you are challenged to balance compliance and creativity, taking initiative, and not stepping on toes. In dealing with trauma, leaders struggle to find a happy medium between being too cautious or too oblivious when a team member is hurting. Do you speak or stay silent? Do you respect their private matters, or do you intervene? As organizations, we struggle to balance stability and growth, spending on technology or human development, focusing on the present or the future. Establishing a balance between extremes for leaders is as difficult as a 65-year-old man striking the Warrior III yoga position.

**The Challenge**

The challenge in Tough Times is to pivot to the next normal. We cannot stay in the trauma but mut do everything we can to make the transition into the better days. But how can we?

The answer is to purposely shift our perspective and vision to what is coming, instead of where we have been. Sometimes all we can do is move one foot while the other stays anchored. We would love leap or run, but we are partially paralyzed by the trauma. It may be a personal tragedy or an organizational challenge or even a worldwide pandemic. No matter what the situation, we need to take whatever steps possible to look and move forward. Often that requires in one small move, a pivot. First, we turn our heads and direct our vision to find the opportunities. Then we move just one foot. That is our first move. From there we can sense and seize the best opportunities.

**The Process**

This book is designed to help you become a pivotal leader, quickly shifting to capitalize on the best opportunities in the Next Normal. The critical first step to pivot your own life and your organization to the New Next Normal. The second critical step is to build a culture that continually fosters innovation, pushing you forward by tracking the trends to anticipate the next opportunity. That also works to make you and your organization resilient to the Tough Times. You will survive because you make pivoting a habit while others are panicking. You will thrive while others are struggling to survive.

**Next Normal**

The term "New Normal" was used extensively during the Covid pandemic to help people understand that we couldn't just go back to what we had before. The shutdown wasn't just a brief interruption but rather a tipping point into a new normal. However, that term implies that we only enter a new normal during the most extreme of disruptions. Instead, Pivotal Leaders understand the need to constantly swivel to the next opportunity. This creates a willingness to change and a habit of frequently changing into a new normal.

The better term is "Next Normal" to identify process of continually looking for "What's next?" We pivot to the next normal every day when we wake up. Wise leaders begin that pivot as they leave work the day before and when they plan strategically for the short and long term. Successful leadership requires pivoting to "What's next?"

Unfortunately, too many in leadership positions are focused on a different question, "What happened?" Notice the pivot to focus the past. Tough Times often leave us wondering "What happened?" and too often "Why?" or "Why me?" Those questions are valid but only briefly. We cannot allow our focus to remain on the past. Instead, we must, as quickly as we can, pivot to looking forward by asking, "What's next?"

The next normal is where our opportunities reside, not in the past. While we are tempted to look back, too often that only leads to the blame and shame game. Let's face it, that game rarely helps anyone. Instead, the Pivotal Leader finds the best opportunities by pivoting to the Next Normal. The key is to make the pivot to the Next Normal a habit.

If we are honest with ourselves, each day is a new normal. Even before we go to bed the evening before, we anticipate the opportunities, knowing the current day's opportunities are past. Each day brings a new beginning while ending the previous one. The changes are often so minor that we often don't recognize the difference.

The Next Normal takes the New Normal to another level. It implies a progression to something new and more permanent. There is a hint of something more dramatic and even traumatic. Most see the Next Normal after an important loss or a significant strategic decision to make a paradigm shift. Our approach to the Next Normal can be positive or negative depending upon why we are making the shift. Those losing a loved one, business, or livelihood, go kicking and screaming into the Next Normal. Even those who make the strategic decision to shift may not be entirely excited about it. No matter the emotions, the Next Normal is the upcoming stage that we cannot avoid. We must take that step because circumstances prevent returning to our Old Normal.

The Next Normal implies that we must find a new pattern of living that brings a sense of comfort, safety, and predictability for ourselves and our team.

**Leadership**

Thousands of books on leadership are written every year. So why would I write another one? I write to help take aspiring and emerging leaders to audacious levels. Solopreneurs and small business owners do not have the resources that large corporations offer. To complicate matters, they don't have the same time and resources larger companies offer their management teams. Meanwhile, they are working as long or even longer hours.

My purpose is to help expand their vision, trigger their thinking, and assist them in reaching higher. In that process, I focus on four aspects: setting audacious but attainable goals, honing established and innovative skills, attaining cutting-edge knowledge, and developing the ultimate attitude.

## PIVOTAL LEADERS

One of the critical skills that is overlooked in current books is the ability to consistently change to focus on the best opportunities in the future. My business partner call that being pivotal. It is one thing to make a single change but a different mindset to become pivotal. This book is focus on becoming more pivotal.

Having studied and taught leadership courses in graduate programs, there are obviously many iconic leadership books. A short list includes titles from Dale Carnegie, Warren Bennis, John C. Maxwell, Jim Collins, Ken Blanchard, Stephen Covey, Simon Sinek, Adam Grant, Daniel Pink, Brené Brown, Sheryl Sandberg, Renée Mauborgne, and Sally Hogshead. Did I miss one of your favorites?

Becoming a great leader is like putting together a 5000-piece jigsaw puzzle that is continually changing. We can't just use rely upon one author to guide us through a world that is changing rapidly and radically. A diversity of perspectives is required.

Some argue that the key to leadership is finding your style and sticking with it. Unfortunately, that doesn't work in the consistently evolving world of work, economics, and politics. Instead, we need to see and leverage a vast diversity of perspectives. The leader must play on their toes, ready to pivot between styles to seize the opportunity of the immediate situation while also focusing on future ones. Pivoting is critical, as you will see in this book, but what we pivot for and to is also critically important.

I have written several books to foster that diversity of leadership perspectives. The books I've written to day work to provide a more complete but not exhaustive approach to leadership. My goal is to help you become the cosmopolitan leader, one who senses and seizes the best opportunities by building the best team in any circumstance. To that end, I've written my first book, *Chevettes to Corvettes* (recently retitled *Pivotal Small Business*) to help develop the Ultimate Leader developing a disruptive business. Too many settle for ordinary when the ultimate is within reach. To this end, a future release will address *Audacious Success*, becoming boldly original and a bit reckless to lead innovation.

Building that team requires becoming a Compassionate Leader, one who comes alongside their team (managers, employees, customers, vendors, and community) to help alleviate their pain. This allows the leader to find the secrets to engaging employees and making more money. (See *Making More Money in Tough Times*, *The ROI of Compassion*, and *Leading with the Power of Compassion*, soon to be retitled *Engage Employees*.) To seize the best opportunities, leaders must be a Thinking Leader, not just reacting, putting out fires, or following what other leaders are doing. (Check out my book *THINK*.) The Thinking Leader prevents the S.T.U.P.I.D. Leader, plagued by stagnant thinking undermining potentially incredible decisions. (*Stop Being S.T.U.P.I.D. in Times of Opportunity*.) Innovative leaders work Inside-Out, understanding the unique value everyone offers. That includes their unique value as well as each team member and extends to how the organization provides unique value to their customers. (*The Prize Inside, Conversations with My Future Self*, volumes I and II.) The Inside-Out Leader is concerned not only about what to do or what to not do, but also who they are. Being is as important as doing. Who we believe ourselves to be will dictate the actions we take and the outcomes we achieve? (Also see *D.I.S.R.U.P.T. Your Listening*, and *D.I.S.R.U.P.T. Your Networking* that will also be retitled shortly into *Pivot your Listening* and *Pivot Your Networking*.)

The cutting-edge leaders have an insatiable appetite for learning and growing. They are bold in their dreams, vision, strategy, and action. To be that leader, we need to become pivotal.

**Pivotal Leadership**

The term "leader" is one that creates misperception. Too many assume that leadership requires a title or at least a team or established team or a group of followers. However, leadership begins with leading yourself. To pivot, requires an inside-out, not just an outside-in process.

Taking the lead requires an internal drive driven by a strong sense of character. You are a leader if you pivot your focus to see the best opportunities in the future. You don't wait for someone to tell you about those opportunities or to go seize them. That is a follower. Instead, the pivotal leader takes the initiative because they have developed the habit of thinking bigger, reaching higher and doing what others won't, can't, or simply don't. They set themselves apart by rising above the circumstances and overcoming challenges others label as "impossible."

# PIVOTAL LEADERS

Leaders don't need to be told what to do. They do reach out to their teams for help and to their advisors for wise counsel. However, leaders take responsibility for their own destiny.

Meanwhile, followers wait to be told and blame others when they don't get what they want. They play it safe, demanding their life be predictable, safe, and comfortable. Followers are frustrated by anything that disrupts their little world.

Notice how the Pivotal Leader is the exact opposite of the follower. Pivotal Leaders seek out disruption. They constantly look to the future, tracking trends, and forecasting opportunities to make the world better. They don't look back blaming and shaming but instead ask, "What's next?" in anticipation.

Also notice that anyone can become a Pivotal Leader. Everyone faces a new day each morning. It doesn't take a title or an official position. You hold the power to shift your focus from the past to the present, and then from the present to the future. You have the power to pivot. You have the power to become pivotal. In that pivotal attitude, you hold the power to shape your world, dictate your success, and claim your destiny.

My passion is to help you transition to a world of seemingly impossible results. I want to help you realize your ultimate dreams, turning the world around you upside in a good way. Create the paradigm shifting innovation. Break through the barriers. Establish the next normal that makes life better by creating products and services that are faster, cheaper, and easier.

> *Most people live Outside-in thinking the world is Right Side-Up when it is actually Upside-Down. It is only when we live Inside-Out that we turn our lives Right-Side Up and their world Upside-Down.*
> Loren Murfield, Ph.D.
> *Pivotal Conversations with Your Future Self*

When events turn our world Upside-Down, our challenge is to live Inside-Out so we can pivot to the Next Normal and seize the best opportunities. We may feel like quitting, but that is the time to start living again. Sense and seize the opportunities that allow you to live 100% alive. Then reach out to others and help them pivot and enjoy the same benefits. What's the alternative? In retrospect, isn't pining for the past pathetic? Appreciate the past, seize the present, and anticipate the future. In the process, learning to pivot and become pivotal will allow you to live beyond your wildest dreams.

**Your Challenge**
What is your biggest challenge in becoming a Pivotal Leader?


NOTE: Each of these principles could be a book in themselves. I've chosen to make each of the chapters concise to initiate bigger thinking and higher action. My goal is to shift your perspective, shedding a new light on important principles that can reveal a brighter vision of the future. While this book can be read quickly, the value is in the contemplation. I suggest reading a chapter a day to allow yourself opportunity to think about and apply the material.

# RECOGNIZING A MAJOR DISRUPTION

Wake Up!
This is a Major Disruption
Whatever situation you are facing today, whether it be the Covid pandemic, the loss of a job, possessions, or a loved one, this is a major disruption.

Forget the old normal.

It's never coming back.

That's what happens with major disruptions. It might be growing older at a senior citizen, losing your health or freedom, or as someone much younger celebrating a benchmark birthday at 30, 40 or 50. Each of these transitions leave behind a normal life and cause a bit of trepidation for the future.

We must realize that we cannot go back. Too much has already changed. It will never be as it once was. Our only hope is to disrupt our thinking to sense and seize the best opportunities in this Next Normal.

**The Problem**

As I write this, we are coming out of the Covid pandemic. But that is not the only transition we make in life, especially as leaders. Every day we as leaders face a number of situations that demand we shift our focus and continue to see the future opportunities. The daily, if not hourly, fires must be extinguished. If we don't address them wisely, they will dictate our choices in the future.

Too many consider trauma or Tough Times as "something awful interrupting our lives." The truth is that Tough Times happen to everyone. No one escapes them. Like the daily fires we extinguish at work, our Tough Times are a part of life itself.

Tough Times are those significant shifts when the bottom drops out of our normal lives. We probably didn't see those Tough Times coming and weren't prepared. Or we saw them coming but underestimated the impact. Tough Times rock our world in the wrong way.

Yet they are a part of everyone's lives. No one escapes the Tough Times. Even though we would rather enjoy the peace and prosperity of good times, Tough Times are normal. Periodic shifts from good to bad and back to good happen to everyone in every age. The challenge we face is to not edit out the Tough Times.

But that's what we do. Why wouldn't we? We enjoy the good times and, when the good times continue, we get complacent in our thinking. We presume all will continue when we know better.

For example, I live in Florida. We know hurricanes are a persistent threat every year. After 2004 when four hurricanes struck the state, everyone was on guard. The next year Katrina skirted the state to the west. Then, for the next decade, west central Florida watched as the hurricanes either didn't develop or went elsewhere. Although we knew better, we started to let our guard down. Sooner or later a hurricane would strike. That sooner came in 2007 as Hurricane Irma caused nearly one third of the population to evacuate.

Cyclical trends don't go away. That was a lesson I learned growing up on a farm in South Dakota. Each season offered tremendous opportunities and dangers. Our winters were brutal with temperatures falling to -20 at some point. Add a stiff wind and significant snowfall and you have a significant threat. Never-the-less, there were chores to be done summer or winter. Dad milked cows and that required considerable preparation. During the summer, we filled the hay loft with feed for the winter. Failure to prepare meant a big problem in the winter. During the winter, milking and caring for the cows added work. A wise farmer prepared his thinking for that work.

Despite dreading the winters, that taught me that life is filled with pleasure and problems. While I loved the lazy days of summer, I knew winter was coming. Even when I moved to Florida to escape the brutal

South Dakota winters, I knew that oppressive summer heat and humidity fostered severe thunderstorms and hurricanes. No matter where you go, you can't escape difficult weather. The only choice we have is to be prepared. We must develop a pivotal mindset where we are constantly willing to look beyond the current situation to the Next Normal.

### *Death, Illness and Fear.*

The Coronavirus struck quickly in the spring of 2020. Businesses shut down. Workers scrambled to learn how to work virtually. Churches, restaurants, and bars shut down. Hospitals feared the worst as they struggled to fight this novel virus. With numbers mounting, no one could confidently predict when the virus would subside. Scientists scrambled to create a vaccine and then attain herd immunity. Meanwhile, the virus spread and killed over 500,000 in the U.S. by the end of the first year.

The pandemic disrupted our lives, requiring us to change almost all our habits. We had to wear masks, maintain a physical distance, and cancel vacations. The pandemic instilled fear, ignited panic, and triggered hoarding. Even a year later as states start to relax their restrictions, the fear can be felt. Many reported feeling anxious when they returned to public, even when wearing a mask and social distancing. They are tired of Zoom conversations. Many wondered, "when will we feel safe again?

Look back and notice the challenges we faced and how we were required to pivot.

### *Business Adaptations, Struggle, and Failure*

Business was scared, fearing the economic recovery wouldn't be fast enough. Six months into the shutdown, 100,000 small businesses had closed forever. Major retailers such as Pier 1 Imports and Garden Restaurants closed. Niemen Marcus, J Crew and True Religion filed for Chapter 11 bankruptcy. Others worked feverishly to find a way to survive.

To prevent the worst of the pandemic, businesses scrambled to quickly transition into virtual work. Workers struggled to balance work and family life as the schools also transitioned to the virtual world. That led to a demand by workers. According to an INC.com survey, percent of Americans want to keep remote work as their primary mode of work. Seventy percent say they'd like it to at least be an option. Fast forward to the spring of 2021, and that sentiment still held as many companies brought back workers into the office. That caused some traditional businesses to tremble at the thought of a permanent shift to the virtual workplace, wondering, "What will the New Normal look and feel like?" They wondered if and how it would work. Some wondered if they even wanted it to work. That generated the question, "What is the future of work?"

### *Racial Unrest*

Amidst the pandemic, old problems of racial prejudice arose with police causing the unnecessary death of more black men. Protests and riots ripped apart cities across the country. Although this isn't the first time, there is an urgency that indicates this will be the last time. Demands for change would not be denied. That caused fear among the established leaders.

It didn't matter whether you claimed, "Black Lives Matter" or "Blue Lives Matter." The same question needed to be asked, "Is the New Normal the same Old Normal?" The follow up question was equally as important, "How can we get to that New Normal?"

### *Technological Disruption*

Meanwhile the changes many have been warning about have been accelerated. Artificial Intelligence and Automation were pushed into service to limit personal contact, providing employers a viable long-term option for human labor. New technology did create higher level jobs, but many workers were not prepared in their thinking patterns. Their stagnant thinking prevented embracing the training to seize the best opportunities.

### **The Cancelation Culture**

Amidst the cultural backlash, cultural icons were suddenly questioned. Dr. Seuss books were banned. Speakers were disinvited from college campuses. Statues were destroyed by angry mobs. Later, due to public scrutiny, Civil War statues were removed. Even a statue of Abraham Lincoln was vandalized.

Several wondered, "What is acceptable in the New Normal?"

# PIVOTAL LEADERS

### *Political Division*

Political division had been growing since the 1980s but the ideological wrangling from both political extremes spread a thinking virus across the country. "Mah Rights" conservatives felt violated when required to wear a mask. They boycotted Costco and claimed imaginary constitutional rights. Fueled by Q-Anon self-serving lies, they cried "conspiracy theory" when anyone criticizes their president.

Meanwhile, the other party sat tight, doing little to fill the void. They offered a few new ideas, but no great leaders stepped forward with innovative solutions. Sadly enough, many politicians only sought to be reelected instead of solving the significant problems.

January 6th of 2021 erupted into a staged coup, conservatives rushed the U.S. Capital seeking to overturn the presidential election. Four hundred arrests were made. Meanwhile, the president did little to quell the violence. Instead, clinging to a falsehood that the election was rigged. Even since the assault, the divide exists, and if possible, continues to grow.

No matter which side of the political divide you stand on, we must ask, "How can we survive as a country with this political division?

### *Distrust of Science and Authority*

At a time when we needed science to lead the way, flatten the pandemic curve, and find a vaccine solution, the president and his followers cast doubt on scientific rigor. Instead, they built policy on their ideological opinions and fostered division when we needed unity. Antivaxxers clung to their favored conspiracy theories over proven facts. When the vaccine did come out, many vehemently refused it. Reasonable people asked, "Is this the New Normal? Can we survive if people no longer trust science? Can we survive if this distrust is spread to every other organizational authority?" These questions pushed many to the brink, wondering, "Are we headed for anarchy? Is this the end of the United States as we know it?"

### *Self-Centered Entitlement*

The entitled fractionalization is the most troubling trend. It began with the Baby Boomers and is widespread among the Millennials and Gen Z. At first, COVID was considered as an "old people" problem.

Younger generations flooded into Florida for 2020 spring break, claiming they were safe. The generations that were thought to be more compassionate turned out to be only concerned for their own enjoyment. Public safety was an inconvenience. Because of that, the U.S. lagged behind the world in recovering from this pandemic. We must ask, with our younger generations behaving like that, "What does the future hold?"

### *Unwillingness to Disrupt Ourselves*

Dig deeper and you find an unwillingness to disrupt ourselves. In general, we refuse to learn how to think bigger or reach higher. It isn't a matter of whether we are able but that we are not willing.

- Too many people expect that life will be easy, and when it is not, that someone else solves the problems for them.
- Too many want to ignore their responsibility to live together in harmony, failing to show compassion for another's pain.
- Too many claim they shouldn't have to change, believing the new way violates moral standards.
- Too many others fail to step up into the leadership void, choosing instead to settle for the lesser of two poor choices.
- Too many blindly listen to news outlets that pander to emotions instead of unbiased truth.

We must ask, "How can we expect to transition into the Next Normal when we aren't willing to bend, adapt, and prepare ourselves? How can we expect to seize the best of New Normal opportunities when we maintain our outdated manner of thinking?"

### Other Tough Times

Don't be lured into thinking that the pandemic was the only time we show this flawed thinking. It happens during many difficult situations. Look back to the 2007-8 recession and you will see evidence of it. The leaders of my networking group wore buttons proclaiming, "I'm not participating in the Recession." Duh. As if we had a choice? They felt they could just deny its existence, and everything would be fine. We can't just deny Tough Times. If we could, we would.

Losing a loved one is one of the worst things that we endure. I've lost an adult son and know many who have lost children. Sudden deaths stop us in our tracts whether it is accident, murder, or suicide. Losing a loved one shatters our future as we picture them growing up and having families. Then there is losing parents. We expect it but still struggle to adapt our thinking. Too often we look back and wish for happier days. Unfortunately, that isn't an option.

**The Tragic Outcome**

Too many cannot move through the tragedy because they cannot see a world without that loved one or lifestyle. They refuse to move on because they believe the old normal was what they deserved or were promised. No wonder they are stuck. They are debilitated by the failure to pivot to the Next Normal. They cannot see the future because they are so focused on the past. Without that vision, they are frozen while the world moves forward. That's tragic because they will never realize the phenomenal opportunities yet to come.

**The Solution**

First, understand that you are in an era of disruption.

Believe it. Accept it.

Any trauma isn't just a hiccup where we return to our old way of living. Those days are gone. Denying it is happening won't change it. Forgive me if that sounds cruel. As stated earlier, I have lost a son and know many who have lost a child. We would do almost anything to bring them back. Many of us couldn't see how we could go on. But in the end, life does go on. There will be a tomorrow despite what happened today. The sooner we embrace that idea, the better off we will be. It doesn't mean we don't appreciate what we lost. It simply means we are willing to live again.

Second, change your attitude. Be willing to learn. Re-examine your beliefs and values. Seriously consider what you need to change in your life to welcome new opportunities. We willing to explore the Next Normal instead of clinging to the past.

Third, learn to think bigger. Use critical thinking to analyze what you read and hear. Question authority. Double check sources. Don't try to solve complicated problems with a simple explanation. Dig for the facts and the details. Just because they hold a title, an office, or a position of influence does not mean that they are right. Also, don't trust anything your read just because it reinforces what you believe.

Test the information. Never before have we had so many ways to check the facts.

Fourth, learn to think compassionately. We are all in this together. Notice the pain of others. Feel for them from their perspective. But don't just empathize, be compassionate by thinking through what you can do to alleviate their pain. Then do it. Take the action.

Fifth, reach higher. We are not doing good enough to flatten the curve of the pandemic or live together in peace. Speak out against injustice. Speak out to ask the critical questions. Speak out to challenge those who refuse to disrupt themselves.

But speak out in a spirit of collaboration, not competition. Get involved. Volunteer to help. Be willing to lead. There is a tremendous opportunity to lead in turbulent times. You don't have to have all the answers but be willing to lead the search for answers. When we are good people and we work collaboratively with other good people, we can do great, not just good, things. Don't settle for the lesser of two poor choices but set the standard and work to exceed it. Reach higher not lower.

The New Normal has incredible opportunities IF we are willing to think bigger and reach higher.

Are you going to go forward, disrupting yourself? If so, you will be in demand, sought out for your discernment and wise decisions.

Or are you going to wait and see? If so, be ready to be disrupted, discounted, and diminished.

If you are willing to go forward, you will need to learn how to pivot. More importantly, you will need to become pivotal, continually shifting to see the next, great opportunity.

**Your Challenge**

Which of the above-mentioned obstacles are your biggest challenges?

# MAKING YOUR PIVOTAL CHANGE

As noted, before, the world is changing rapidly and radically. Some like the change while others hate it. Still others deny it while the pivotal leader welcomes it. What is your attitude about change?

**Change**

The world changes every day. Like it or not, believe it is good or bad, but every day the world changes in some way every day. The challenge we have as leaders is to deal with the continual change.

Each day brings a new sunrise but also a slightly different world. What happened yesterday is history and new opportunities will emerge today. A significant part of those opportunities emerges through our attitude. Yesterday's frustrations vanish with a good night's sleep. The persisting challenges linger but you can approach them with renewed energy and perspective. New challenges and opportunities will appear. If we welcome each with a focus on the opportunity rather than the frustration, we learn, grow, and enjoy the benefits. If we treat each instance as yet another inconvenience that detracts from what we want, that's what we will experience.

Many live Outside-In thinking the world is upside-down. They feel "put upon" by external events. But when they (we) learn to live Inside-Out, changing our perspective to see opportunities instead of obstacles, we turn our world right side up and that outside world upside-down. Our attitude about change dictates the opportunities we perceive. The old adage, "garbage in-garbage out" prevails. What we think is what we become.

# PIVOTAL LEADERS

**Who Are You?**

I recently met the musician Craig Richard whose favorite quote is, "We don't see the world as it is, we see it as we are." At an early age, he discovered the joy of rock climbing from his father and the love of music from his mother. In 2006 he and his cousin Ken Sherbenou were training to climb the fabled peak, El Capitan in Yosemite National Park. They traveled to the remote Black Canyon in Colorado where they would repel 1000 feet down into the canyon in order to climb back up. Everything was working according to plan. Then, halfway up the climb, an anchor slipped, and yelled, "I'm falling." Fortunately, the ropes prevented a fatal flaw. Unfortunately, he was in pain. He knew he hit his leg and didn't know the extent of the problem. Determined to keep going, he tried to stand but quickly collapsed. He had broken his leg below the knee. Trying to stand proved to be excruciating as the bones broke and the broken ends slipped alongside each other.

At that point, the climb was done. If he were to continue, he had another six hours of climbing to get out of the canyon. Without that option, he had to retreat down the canyon and then crawl out the way they came in. However, that was no easy trek. Remember, they repelled into the canyon. They slowly inched their way down the cliff face and plotted their route up the other side, which was less challenging but still formidable. By now they were tired, hungry, and thirsty. Their supplies exhausted as well as their strength, Craig crawled on his hands and knees for three hours with a broken leg. Meanwhile, his cousin Ken, set the attitude. (to hear the entire story, go to PivotalCareerGrowth.com/podcasts and look for the episodes featuring Craig Richards.)

In such a time, you might expect a compassionate tone, continually asking how he is faring. But that's not what Ken did because that wasn't their relationship. Instead, they busted on each other. Ken teased Craig with, "You will never get a date now. Women don't want to date a cripple." He kept the mood light knowing that would give Craig energy and pivot his mindset from obstacle to opportunity. Craig said in our podcast an interview, that made the difference in taking the tenacious action to spend 18 hours climbing out of canyon with a broken leg.

When asked for his favorite quote, he quickly noted "we don't see the world as it is, we see it as we are." We become what we think about. That pivot from outside-in to inside-out turns obstacles into opportunities. You might be surprised to learn that Craig was back climbing just a month later with a cast on his leg. The next year he successfully climbed El Capitan.

Are you focusing on the opportunity or the frustration?
Who are you?
Who are you in this moment?
Who are you willing to become to seize the best opportunities?

*"We don't see the world as it is, we see it as we are."*
Anaïs Nin

The action we take will reveal our attitude about change. At the same time, we can change our attitude to become pivotal agents of change.

**Attitude about Change**
Attitude has two critical elements: beliefs and values. Beliefs are what we hold to be true. For example, we all believe the sun rises in the east each morning. Whether we see it or not, we know the sun rises each morning. Technically, we know the earth is rotating and not the sun but our belief holds. When we go to bed at night, we know the sun will rise over the horizon welcoming a new day.

We often base our beliefs based on scientific evidence, personal experience, tradition, or personal opinion.

What do you believe about change?
Do you believe change is generally good?
Or do you believe change is harmful and should be avoided?

A value is something that we consider so significant that we build our lives upon it. We value hard work because we have seen how it makes life better. The same can be said for accountability, flexibility, and personal initiative. Some value comfort over hard work, favoring enjoyment over potential results.

How much do you value change?
Comfort is good but do you value change enough to make your life uncomfortable?

Are the opportunities you envision worth the effort to change your attitude and behavior?

Values are revealed by your behavior, not just your language.

## Stages of Change

James Prochaska and Carlo DiClemente researched health-related behavior change (Prochaska & DiClemente, 1983). They detailed a model to assess an individual's readiness to act for the purpose of eliminating a problem behavior. Their Stages of Change Model is widely accepted and gives us a valuable insight into becoming pivotal leaders.

As you read this chapter, focus on three perspectives.

1. Identify which stage represents your attitude about a general sense of change.

2. Identify the stage that best represents your attitude about a specific change you are facing.

3. Identify the stage that best represents your potential customer's or your team member's attitude about change.

Note: For ease of reading and understanding, I've changed the names of each stage to spell out P.I.V.O.T.

## P- Play Dumb

The first stage of change, and the worst attitude about change is denying the need for change. or simply not being aware of change. In many ways, this is a euphoric stage where we are oblivious to any consequences from not changes. We ignore the trends and don't think about the opportunities of the future.

Listen to your language and you will hear yourself say the following phrases.

"I don't see how life can get any better than this."
"It's not going to get that bad. They are making too much out of it."
"Why should we change?"
"We've never done it that way before."
"Let's just continue on with the plan we have."

Many don't see a need for change, in part because they don't want to make the effort to leave their comfortable status quo. Part of the denial is a stubbornness to realize change can be good. Some villainize change. They purposely don't track the trends because they believe nothing can be better than what they have right now. When honest, many times they (we) deny change because we are afraid of what will happen.

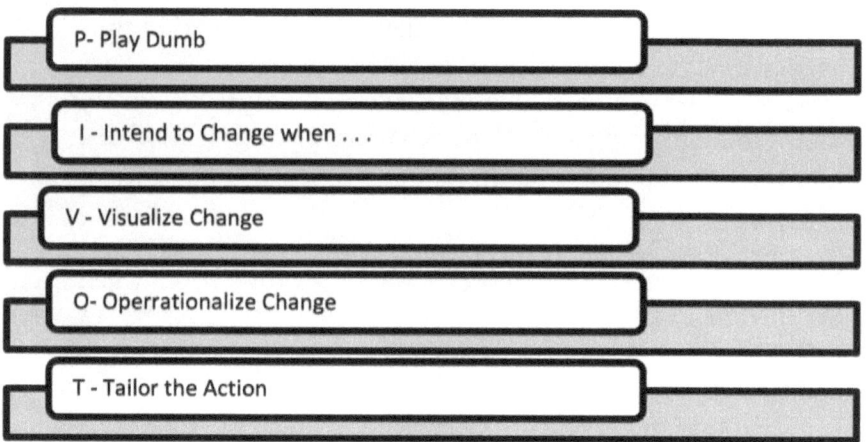

Other times people are simply unaware because they are so busy working in the moment to pay the bills. It is easy to become unaware, oblivious to the consequences and the opportunities when we sequester ourselves from reality. Become aware of the potential.

Sometimes, as we have seen recently, change becomes political. They deny the facts in favor of reinforcing their opinions. "It isn't happening.' "They are lying." "I don't care what the facts say, I feel better when I . . .."

Change is the freight train coming through the tunnel. It's not stopping or slowing down because of your opinion.

Note: I'm not claiming that every new idea is good and should be adopted. Instead, my goal is to help you identify your attitude about change and recognize the consequences if you fail to change that attitude.

As leaders in any industry but especially real estate, sales, and business, we deal with deniers or the unaware every day. We can help educate the unaware but are wise to avoid the deniers. Don't spend your energy trying to convince them. There are far better opportunities.

# PIVOTAL LEADERS

*"Only the wisest and stupidest of men never change."*
Confucius, Chinese Philosopher

## I – Intention

The second stage of change is thinking about changing but not yet committed. We like the idea but aren't quite ready to commit to the change.

Listen to your language, and theirs. If you hear any of the following, you are hearing this stage.

"I like the idea, but . . ."

"The thing you have to understand is, . . ."

"What does _____ think about this?"

"I need to research this further."

"I'm just not ready to make a decision."

Intention is much better than denial or being unaware. With intention, there is a positive approach to change but not the commitment.

When you find yourself, potential customer, or team member in the Intention stage, ask the following questions.

"What do you/I need to make the commitment?"

"What consequences will happen if you/I don't take the action now?"

"What benefits will you/I receive if we commit right now?"

*"Indecision may or may not be my problem."*
Jimmy Buffett

## V- Visualize

The third stage of change is the preparation stage, where we become ready to make a change. I like the label "visualize" because it engages the mind to focus on the future. At this stage, we don't just dream, we focused intently, churning through the possibilities and the plans to seize a particular opportunity. Visualizing, in this sense, is preparing your mind to make the change.

Listen to the language of visualization.

"I can see it."

"To make this happen, we need to _____."

"This will be fun/good/productive."

Notice there is a pivot in the language. You are not looking back, but to the future. At this point, you know you can't return to the past and don't want to. Instead, you have turned and are emotionally ready to take the leap into the future.

Ask yourself the following questions when in this stage of change.

"What am I seeing?"
"What do I need to do to make this dream a reality?"
"Where do I begin?"
"Who do I need to help me?"
"How soon can I start?"

*I visualize things in my mind before I have to do them. It's like having a mental workshop.*
Jack Youngblood, NFL Hall of Fame Player

## O- Operationalize

The fourth stage of change is to act. This is where you put the plan from the visualization stage into action. In many ways, this requires the least amount of explanation. Like Nike's slogan, "Just Do It!" The time for thinking is done, now is the time to take the necessary action.

Language heard in this stage is:
"Let's do it."

That's it. It's all about execution. Taking exactly the right action at the perfect time to the standard expected.

Notice that procrastination is a failure to act. Procrastinating delays action based on a fear.

Ask yourself the following questions in this stage of change.
"What action is needed?"
"Why am I not doing it right now?"
"What am I afraid of?"

Quit thinking. Quit feeling. Take the necessary action at the appropriate time.

*"The path to success is to take massive, determined action."*
Tony Robbins

## T - Tailor

The fifth and final stage of change is maintenance or, adapting. I prefer the word "tailor" not only because it spells out "pivot" but because it requires personalization. Change requires adapting to the specific individual or situation. It is personal and even intimate. As we take the action, we must monitor our actions to the specific opportunity in front of us. We also must fine-tune our actions to perfect the subsequent results. That requires assessing our action, performing the necessary maintenance to perfect our process.

Notice the continual pivot in that tailoring adaptation. Tailoring creates a habit of being pivotal. To pivot is good but to continually tailor our approach to change is even better. That creates an attitude of anticipating the need for change, visualizing the potential and then taking the action.

In sales or leadership, we must always be looking to adapt to the individual, market, and conditions. While some things may stay the same, we cannot expect the same old, comfortable position. Instead, we must be on our toes, alert to nuances that will bring us that audacious level of success.

Tailoring your language to develop a pivotal attitude.
"What can I do to perfect my performance?"
"How can I be more efficient?"
"How can I increase my results?"
"Where can I expand my reach?"
"Who else can I help?"

*"In fast moving fields like cancer, where doctors tailor treatments based on evidence that's constantly evolving, two years can be an eternity of waiting to learn about important science. For some patients, that interval can be fatal."*
Scott Gottlieb

## Your Challenge:

THINK BIGGER: Embrace the benefits of continual change.
REACH HIGHER! Make the commitment and design your plan.
DO THE IMPOSSIBLE: Continually dare to do what others won't, can't, or simply don't. That will set you into elite results.

# 21 PRINCIPLES

*PIVOTAL LEADERS*

# 1. TRACK THE TRENDS – FORECAST THE OPPORTUNITIES

Whenever trauma happens, it stuns us and we wonder, "What just happened?" We quickly ask the follow-up question, "What does it mean?"

Remember what it felt like in March of 2020 at the beginning of the COVID19 shutdown. Most of the world was forced into quarantine. Amazon, Microsoft, and Expedia sent employees home to work. Harvard and University of Washington were the first to convert all classes to online. My grandson's first grade class in Bothell, Washington was the first school district to convert to online. Initially it was for only two weeks. Little did they know it would be for more than a year.

Remember how we as a culture asked, "What does this mean? When will we return to normal? Will we ever get back to normal? If so, when?"

But as we crept deeper into the shutdown, traditional leaders were faced with a more specific and unsettling question, "Could we be seeing a linear trend toward the virtual workplace?"

In this chapter we will discuss six trends that will disrupt every business in the next five years. No one will escape these disruptions.

**Disruptive Trends**

The disruption is coming. It won't be just a minor change but a radical change that radically alters the way we see the world. That disruption has and will continue to cause tremendous pain. "Will you be on the cutting edge or the bleeding edge of that disruption?"

Daniel Burris delineates linear from cyclical trends in Flash Foresight (2011). We discussed cyclical trends, like the farming seasons, in the previous chapter. They are reliable patterns that we can predict. Linear trends don't repeat. Instead, leaders are challenged to predict where they will take us.

An example of a linear trend is telephone technology. The trend started when Alexander Graham Bell invented the telephone in 1876. As the invention spread, people relied on it with the same constraints for over a century. The first mobile phone was released in 1973. As costs dropped and technology increased, it to cut the cord tethering us to our home phones in the 1990s. The next step in this linear trend was the Blackberry. With its 1999 release, we had access to emails wherever we had a signal. The release of the iPhone took us further as we had access to the internet. We could run a business from anywhere in the world with a signal.

Notice, unlike a cyclical trend, we didn't go back or repeat any part of the trend.

The challenge is to predict the next step.

Currently there are six major trends that will disrupt every business in the next few years. These aren't the only trends but the ones we will discuss are the ones that will challenge every business leader. Our challenge is to mentally prepare by tracking the trend and forecasting the opportunity. That process will help you create a cutting-edge vision and prepare your team for the future. That's when you create a cutting-edge culture that creates the disruption, not be displaced by it.

**Your Focus**

Notice the challenge? To lead your organization, you want to be on the cutting-edge, those who are creating the disruption. That is far better than following what others do and being blown about by the winds of change. We lead in the Next Normal by looking to the future, not the past. Our focus creates our vision.

Where is your focus?

# PIVOTAL LEADERS

**Your Attitude**

Let me ask you a few questions about one trend: virtual work. Be honest and answer with a simple yes or a no.

Do you believe more work will be done virtually in the future?
Do you think the trend applies to your business?
Do you like the trend?
Do you believe the old way was better?

No matter what answer you gave, it doesn't matter. Are you surprised?

The trend is happening whether you like it or not. The trend is happening whether you believe it or not. Whether you see these trends as right, wrong, or indifferent doesn't change anything. The trends are happening. Your leadership challenge is to track the trends and forecast the opportunities. Along with that, you will calculate the consequences if you don't change.

That might not sound very compassionate, but it is. The pain I'm trying to help you alleviate is being disrupted like Blackberry was. They refused to change and now where are they?

**Forecasting Opportunities**

The trends show that the following trends are linear and leading us away from where we are currently. The disruption is coming, and many are not prepared. But imagine the opportunities when you identify what others will need – before they need it. That is forecasting the opportunities.

## PIVOTAL LEADERS

The pivot comes in shifting from seeing a trend as a problem to seeing it as an opportunity. Problems are merely opportunities in disguise. Pivot to see the opportunities in each of the following trends.

Isn't it better to wake up now than live with our heads in the sand and be surprised later? Being proactive trumps being reactive.

### 1. Technology Displacing Jobs

Let's start with the elephant in the room, technology. There is no bigger driver of change today than the rapidly evolving use of technology. Artificial Intelligence and Automation are developed to the point that in the next decade we will see a tremendous loss of jobs in the U.S. and worldwide. As leaders, we must anticipate a radical change in the future of work.

For example, Time.com reports that many of the jobs displaced by the COVID-19 pandemic will be replaced by robots. (Time.com) This follows a trend that manual labor positions can be done better, faster, and cheaper than humans. The good news is that technology will develop millions of jobs in the coming years, but the workers won't be prepared to fill those jobs. (Zdnet.com)

### The Projections

Kai-Fu Lee, author of *AI Superpowers* and former employee at Apple, Microsoft and Google, projects that the technology will displace 40% of all jobs by 2030. Meanwhile, PwC projects a 38% loss of jobs and 44% of all workers without an education will be affected by mid 2030s.

You have read in previous posts how I was a warehouse and factory worker some years ago. Today Amazon uses robots to do what I did as an order-filler in my early adult years. Chatbots are already welcomed instead of calling customer service. Many of us already use Alexa, Google Maps, and facial recognition. Not only are they helping us do what we couldn't otherwise think possible, they are likely displacing some lower-level jobs. Expand your perspective and we see that driverless technology is quickly progressing to the point that it will be noticeable in 202 and completely take over by 2040.

When we look at the projections, we see a world where our old way of work is disappearing rather quickly. The world of work where we did repetitive work over and over is quickly disappearing.

**The Resistance**

Those who believe these dire projections are labeled "future pessimists" because they see the negative. Meanwhile, those who disagree are labeled "future optimists."

There are those who claim these projections are hype and hoax, that jobs won't be destroyed and that jobs will be created as fast as they are lost.

**My Take**

In all my research I have found that most of the experts foresee a significant disruption coming. Not only do leaders like Kai-Fu Lee see a significant loss of jobs, but their projections also make sense. We all want great technology that takes away the pain of repetitive jobs. Business owners want new technology that is better, faster, and cheaper than human labor. Meanwhile, we lack the workers for some jobs like truck drivers and brick layers so new technology is welcomed. I don't see that dissipating any time soon.

Mix that with the leap in progression for AI and we suddenly are at a point where jobs in both blue and white collar will be lost. Look around and we see kiosks to order in fast food restaurants and self-checkout in big box retailers. Extend that experience to office jobs and we see the repetitive work of transactional law and mortgage underwriting both being disrupted soon. Our current experience affirms what the experts are predicting.

That's where I foresee additional pain and opportunities. Not only will they lose their jobs, but they will also not be of the mindset to progress into jobs created by new technology.

Notice the opportunities for training and retraining programs. If you are a business owner or executive, notice how new technology can cut your expenses and increase your bottom line. Also notice that will enable you and your organization to upgrade your products and services. This may be able to expand your market. The opportunities abound if you are willing to become pivotal.

To successfully navigate this paradigm shift, we must help others to think bigger and reach higher. This is no easy task, and many will excuse themselves from the creative discussion claim they don't have one of three things.

- PROCESS – They don't know how to be creative.
- CONFIDENCE/IDENTITY – They don't think they are a creative person or even that they could be.
- INCENTIVE – They don't think the disruption will happen or that they will be affected by it.

Leaving people to their own devices will create tremendous pain for themselves and others. Sadly, those people make up the majority of the workforce.

## Compassionate Leadership – Anticipating the New Pain

Those of us who are willing to track this trend and forecast the opportunities (as well as the threats) must be bold. This is no task for the weak. To solve the serious problems, we must do what we have never done before. We must become disruptive leaders and build cutting-edge teams to do what we used to think was impossible. That means all of us must step up our game. Here are three suggestions.

1. Observe and listen to each team member. What do they need to become a creative thinker and then a disruptive leader?

2. What incentive can you give them to do what they have never done before?

3. How can you build their confidence?

## 2. Growing Consumer Involvement

We all have more power as consumers and companies are realizing how much power customers really have. As leaders, we must anticipate a shift in the way we operate our companies to maintain and grow.

Transparency and customer engagement drive business today. It is a trend that is already greatly impacting businesses and will continue to grow. If you think you can hide, you are in for a big surprise.

**The Trend**

There was a day that doesn't seem that long ago where we didn't have much of a voice. Maybe that was because we didn't have Smart Phones or the Internet or even email. I know, for some of you that seems ancient but that was only 30 years ago. (Not that long in the history of the world.) That technology has given each of us a voice where once we had none.

Think about what it was like. If we received poor customer service, what did we do? We could tell our friends but only by talking to them in person or via a landline, rotary dial phone. We could write to the newspaper hoping it would be published.

But today everything has changed. If we are dissatisfied, we can tweet, blog or post. We can post a video of the bad service or even go live while at the business location. If our post has the right reaction, it can go viral. Where once we had no voice, today we have an immensely powerful voice.

So what?

This should scare us as Pivotal Leaders.

Why?

Because we can no longer hide from bad reviews. Customers can now dictate how we run our business with the threat of walking away and taking other customers with us.

That should frighten and encourage every one of us, even if we don't own the company. As employees, our jobs are on the line. One bad day could spoil years of work. On the other hand, this is a great way to build our credibility.

That sounds harsh. Am I exaggerating? Just ask United Airlines. They are still reeling, years later, from the viral video of a doctor being beaten and dragged off the plane for no fault of his own.

Let's look at our own behavior.

When was the last time you were extremely disappointed in a service provider?

- Did you send out a tweet? Post? Blog?
- Did you message your friends?
- When did you send it?
- Did you post a negative review?

I recently returned from a business trip to Las Vegas and went to a highly rated restaurant. They pride themselves on perfection, so we anticipated legendary service. Unfortunately, they fell short on several points. The wine arrived after the food course, my salmon was dry despite specific instructions for a medium heat and the waiter was not to be found. What did I do? I drew their attention to it at the time and then posted on the 3rd party reservation site. Of course, you notice I'm also writing about it. I'm being nice and not mentioning the name of the restaurant because you would recognize it. However, most won't be that nice.

What would you have done?

Notice the power we have as consumers?

## Capitalizing on the Trend

What can we do to capitalize on this trend?

Engage your customers. See them as part of your company. That doesn't mean just adding them to your email list so you can blast out the special offers. No, engage them. Listen to their pain. Then come alongside of them to alleviate that pain. Work to build a collaboration that creates raving fans. Those that focus on customer engagement and deliver stellar service quickly stand out from the drone of ordinary.

Two nights before we had reservations at Emeril's New Orleans Fish House in Las Vegas. The experience was phenomenal with attentive servers that anticipated our needs. They didn't just drop off the appetizer, entree or dessert but double checked to ensure each was as desired. This was the service we expected. We left a good tip, posted a 5-star review and brag about it to anyone who will listen. Notice I mentioned the name here.

How are you capitalizing on this trend?

**Going Farther**

But the involvement goes much farther than a review. Engage your customers in product development. Identify their pain by asking them what they want and don't want. Engage them with ideas of how to make your products or services better. Give them a voice in your business because they already have one.

How much power are you giving your customers?

**3. Generational Shift**

The Millennials are now the largest generation in the workplace. Gen Z is quickly following. We must embrace the changes they will bring or find ourselves on the outside looking in.

How can Gen Y and Z find their best opportunities in the current workplace?

Here are 3 things you can do as a member of Gen Y or Z that will help you find your ultimate opportunity.

First, Collaborate.

Work to build a spirit of collaboration. As younger workers, I know it is difficult to wait for your opportunity. However, all of those who have come before you have waited their turn. Yes, we also understand that you are not used to waiting. But please, work with those who have come before you. Drop the attitude and embrace the differences. Pivot to become the collaborator, initiating relationships with those in other age groups to learn from them. You might even be surprised that working with them will provide the opportunity you have been waiting for.

Second, Diversify Your World.

You have your own world that is pretty cool. Why hang out with those old folks? I know I get it because I'm one of those old folks that you don't want to work with much less hang with. But consider this. There is a lot of shortcuts you can learn from older workers. Why re-invent the wheel or any other thing? Tap their knowledge and experience by asking about their world. Learn what it took for them to make it. While you won't have to live entirely in that world, there are lessons you can learn from making their world a part of yours.

Third, Show Up.

You won't find any opportunities if you don't show up. The biggest complaint from the older generations have toward Millennials and Gen Z is that they expect too much without providing the effort.

Track this trend and forecast how you can leverage it.

### 4. Growing Fractionalization

The current polarization in politics and culture will continue. As leaders, one of the most difficult tasks will be to recognize the trend and see our opportunities to be peacemakers.

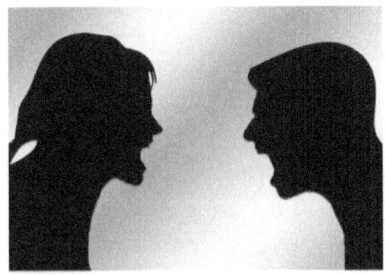

What happened to negotiation or compromise? Everyone seems to have an extreme opinion on every topic. It doesn't matter whether it is religion. politics, or any other issue.

What opportunities can you find in the growing trends of extreme disagreement, otherwise called fractionalization?

It doesn't take a PhD to convince you that our world has been divided into several, very opinionated groups. Our ability to compromise and collaborate has been greatly reduced as our opinions have grown into unwavering ideological beliefs. While I believe there is far more to gain by collaborating, there are incredible opportunities you can tap by focus on the market niche of those factions. Below are six areas where you may find disruptive opportunities. Each of these areas deserve much more discussion. For now, use these questions to help identify your disruptive opportunities.

**Politics**

It doesn't matter which side of the political aisle you support to know that there seems to be no compromise in political support. You are either on one side or the other. While that is often unpleasant, there is tremendous opportunity for making more money. By choosing a side, you are catering to the one ideology and support it.

- Which side do you support?
- What issues do you favor?
- What services or products can you provide that assist them in the efforts?
- How can you be the peacemaker or show each side how to work together?

**Cultural Unrest**

Our world is torn apart with individuals claiming their rights and one group pitted against another group. This creates a increasing tension but also an opportunity to focus on that niche. The choices are identical to the previous group.

- Which side do you support?
- What issues do you favor?
- What services or products can you provide that assist them in the efforts?
- How can you be the peacemaker or show each side how to work together?

**Social Connection**

Never before have we had the ability to connect instantly with so many people around the globe. This has fostered division as those once isolated people can now connect with like-minded individuals outside of their immediate area.

- What niche group do you want to connect with virtually?
- How can you help them further connect or mobilize around their mission?
- What products and service do they need that you offer?

**Willingness to Shatter Norms**

With the technology and cultural disruptions, our social norms are changing quickly. Traditions that have stood for decades or even

centuries are now being shattered. While you might not like the change, that does create new opportunities for products and services.
- What norms/traditions are being shattered that you notice?
- What do people need in building new traditions?
- What products or services do you have, or can you create in the adjustment period?

### Uncivil Communication

There used to be a sense of public and private decorum. That is well gone or at least rapidly waning. However, there are many opportunities when we look at those who want to rise above the fray and communicate effectively.
- How can you be a great example of civil communication?
- How can you foster civil communication in your team?
- What products and services can you provide that help people communicate better?

### Loneliness & Suicide

Despite the many ways to connect virtually, there is an epidemic of loneliness. Oddly enough, the more people spend time online, the more they feel left out. Part of this comes with social judging by others and by ourselves. We see what others are posting and measure ourselves against the public image they project. Right or wrong, a number of people don't feel included.

Maybe that is why the suicide rate has climbed significantly. We lose over 20 U.S. veterans a DAY. We lose 80 individuals between 16 and 24 each week. Women between 45 and 65 are the most vulnerable while men over 65 are especially vulnerable. (NIH.com) There is tremendous opportunity to offer products and services to help the trend of loneliness and suicide.
- What services can you provide to connect those who feel disconnected?
- What services can you create to prevent suicide?
- What products or services can you provide for the families of those who have died?

## 5. Collaborative Leadership

With the Millennials and Gen Z emerging, leadership must become more engaging and collaborative. Businesses must become more transparent and willing to make the world better. If not, the younger generations will find someone else.

That will be the key to disruptive innovation. Will you as a leader be up for the challenge?

Have You Noticed the Growing Trend of Collaborative Leadership? Competition used to be the dominant business model. In fact, it still may be, however, you will see an increasing trend in collaborative leadership. Why? First, technology is making connecting much easier. Second, more leaders are recognizing that we can do more together than we can by ourselves. Third, we are facing bigger problems that demand we work together.

Synergy tells us that great things happen when good people work together. Notice that is good, not necessarily great people achieving great results. 1 + 1 = 3 or 5 or even 11 when leaders bring their best ideas without being takers. When both parties are confident in the relationship, they are free to work together in a generous way. Trust fosters a willingness to try. But beware, if that trust is violated, the collaboration will struggle.

### Mark Cuban and the NBA

In a recent Inc. article, Mark Cuban addresses the trend of players working behind the scenes to build their own championship teams and negotiate record contracts. In the old world, owners would have competed and set rules against those practices. But Mark Cuban suggests a different tactic. (Bariso, 2019)

"This reality has changed what it is like to be an employer," explains Cuban. "In the past, the default was that the best employees would want a long career with their employers, because that is what you did. You kept your job as long as you could. No longer. Now the onus is on employers to keep their best employees happy."

Cuban understands the trends we have discussed in previous posts on the generational shift, technology, customers, and fractionalization. He notices the problems of trying to compete with employees instead of collaborating with them. He also knows that he business and others are far more productive when it is filled with happy workers.

What opportunities do you foresee by collaborating instead of competing?

## 4. Leadership Behaviors

The Harvard Business Review surveyed CEO's and determined four collaborative leadership skills. (HRB.com, 2017)

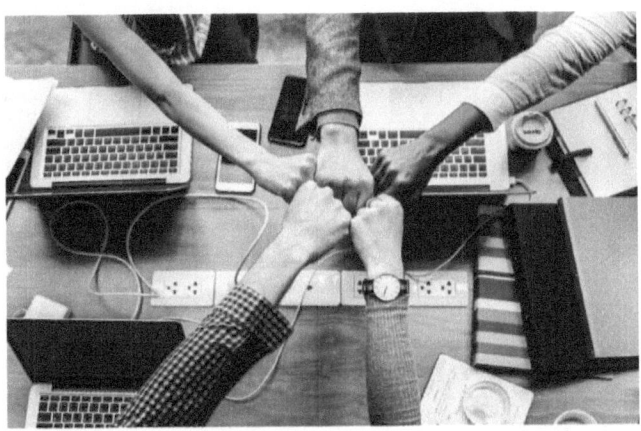

First, they connect people. You have read it before on this site, communication is the life blood of any great organization. Without that connection, the competition cuts the leader off from the human resources they need to create disruptive innovation.

Second, they engage diversity. Disruption doesn't happen when we are content following what we have done before. We need that diversity of thought. What better way to create that diversity of thinking than by hiring team members who think differently?

Third, they build what I call a cutting-edge culture. We all know that organizational culture starts at the top. HRB lists one of the four collaborative skills as collaborating at the top. That means executives model collaboration for the rest of the organization.

Fourth, they maintain the integrity of collaboration. Too many take collaboration too far and acquiesce to employees, giving up too much. Collaboration means pooling your resources to solve the significant problem. Collaboration doesn't mean caving to all of team members requests. It requires a spirit of camaraderie where each willingly offers their best. Remember, collaboration is a win-win. Don't let collaboration become a win-lose competition.

You can choose to be the collaborative leader and be on the cusp of this emerging trend or choose to stand by and watch others build stronger and more productive teams. Imagine the disruptive opportunities you can seize with a shift from competition to collaboration.

## 6. Virtual Work

The numbers are impressive, according to the U.S. Census and Bureau of Labor Statistics data by Global Workplace Analytics, the remote and flexible work consulting firm, and FlexJobs, the virtual workplace is a hard, linear trend. New technology is creating significant opportunities for the virtual workplace.

Since 2005, remote work has grown 216%.

Between 2016 and 2017 remote work grew 7.9%.

Over the last five years, remote work growth is at 44%.

Over the last 10 years remote work has grown 91%.

3.4% of the total U.S. workforce are remote workers, up from 2.9% in 2015.

4.7 million people in the U.S. currently telecommute, up from 3.9 million in 2015.

Since the pandemic, 56% of employees have a job where at least some of the work could be done remotely.

69% of employees worked from home during the pandemic.

82% of employees say they want to work from home after the pandemic.

35% of employees say they would change jobs if offered the opportunity to work remotely fulltime.

## The Value of Working Remotely

Working remotely offers an organization several advantages, according to Flexjobs. (Courtney, Flexjobs.com) It raises employee satisfaction and attracts and retains new talent. Remote workers are more productive, healthier, and make more money. No wonder businesses benefit. That flexibility allows the organization to be nimbler with space, expenses, and strategy. Then consider how that curtails the need for roads, parking, and fuel. The environment also benefits.

The Challenges

Managing your team working virtually requires a different paradigm than the "butts in seats" model. Successful leaders of remote teams require a balance of compassion and accountability.

Compassion is coming alongside another to help alleviate their pain. Leading requires we understand their frustrations and then work to alleviate that barrier to their disruptive success. That is difficult enough when everyone works in the same location.

Working remotely creates new types of pain that managers and leaders must address to deliver disruptive innovation. Unfortunately, many managers focus on compliance rather than compassion. Organizational structure and physical presence trumps employee pain and stifled creativity. The square peg must fit in the round hole. Making that paradigm shift is critical to the virtual workplace succeeding. However, it will be challenging.

Accountability is equally important to compassion because it provides the necessary balance. As explained in *The ROI of Compassion*, too much compassion bankrupts an organization. Everything has limits. Flexibility is great but not if productivity suffers. Employees like independence but not if the goals of the team suffer.

The virtual workplace poses several challenges.

How can you maintain productivity?

How will you know what your team members need?

Do your team members have the physical space to work effectively?

Do they have the emotional safe space at home to work effectively?

Will they be lonely when not connected to the group?

What will it take to maintain team connectivity?

Do they have the discipline to work effectively apart from the office and the other team members?

What policies need to change to foster their success?

What technology will they need?

What technology will you need to manage them?

What paradigms, perspectives, attitudes, practices, policies, and behaviors among management need to change to foster success?

The Tipping Point?

There are many challenges, but this trend is not a matter of "if" but "when?" and "where?" We have reached a point where working from home or any other location is feasible and, in many cases, advisable. (We have probably been there for some time but are only now realizing it.) There are too many benefits for businesses and employees to ignore this trend. This shutdown will convince many who have hesitated that virtual work is a good practice.

However, there are still benefits from person-to-person contact. We will appreciate each of those benefits during this COVID-19 shutdown. Humans are social animals and businesses need personal interaction. But do we need as much as we have had? Probably not. There are ways that we can use technology to make life easier while making business better.

**Your Challenge:**

How can you pivot your thinking and find the opportunities in each of these trends?

# 2: STAY FOCUSED

Whenever trauma strikes, there is a temptation to panic. Panic is defined as "a sudden overwhelming fear, with or without cause, that produces hysterical or irrational behavior, and that often spreads quickly through a group of persons or animals." (Dictionary.com)

Panic is not good for anyone, but people still do it. As leaders in the Next Normal, it is our job to think and behave rationally. The next step is to foster that same mindset with our teams.

My pet peeve is people who react with over-the-top emotion. Upon hearing bad news, they become totally useless, wailing, screaming, and falling to the floor.

Pardon me if that sounds harsh but understand that panic serves no one or any purpose. Panic is simply an emotional outburst.

With that said, a good friend suffers from PTSD following an armed robbery where he was shot five times. One bullet missed his femoral artery by a centimeter. His panic comes from a near death experience. I understand that. In those moments, he needs someone to be reassuring and help him through the moment.

But most panic is simply knee-jerk reaction to what individuals and leaders fear the most. As leaders, our responsibilities rest in creating cutting-edge cultures that are grounded in rational thinking and behavior. We don't respond based on emotion and especially on fear. We track the trends to forecast the opportunities. We are always looking forward except to analyze our most recent performance. Even in that analysis, we are more focused on moving forward than blaming and shaming for past work.

Below are six ways to foster that rational mindset and find the best opportunities in the future.

**#1. It's not as bad as you think.**

Panic is unbridled fear. We fear what could happen. Notice that I said, *could* not *will*.

Panic is a problem with our mindset, a flaw in the way we have been conditioned to think. Lukianoff and Haidt (Lukianoff & Haidt, 2018) list 8 ways we distort our thinking.

- Let your feelings guide your view of reality.
- Focus on the worst possible outcome.
- Believe one incident dictates the future.
- See only good or bad, either/or choices.
- Assume what others are thinking.
- Label ourselves as bad.
- Focus on the negatives and don't see the positives.
- Blame others.

Notice how many of these are what I call Outside-In thinking. We panic when we believe the external events overwhelm our internal strengths. The challenge is to build our Inside-Out thinking as leaders and as cutting-edge teams. When we habitually focus on the opportunities by tracking the trends and looking to the future, we become mentally strong.

Remember as the COVID 19 began, there was a fear of contamination. Even though only 2% were dying of the virus, most of us were extremely cautious because we didn't want to be one of those. So many adopted new habits beyond masks and physical distancing. They sanitized everything brought into the home, including mail and groceries. They also quickly changed and washed their clothes. This was rational behavior based on scientific advice.

Some, however, panicked and started hoarding toilet paper and cleaning supplies. Their panic assumed the worst. By letting their feelings guide their behavior, they imagined running out of toilet paper. In other words, they turned a rational habit into a potential catastrophe. "What will I do?" That led to panic buying and a shortage of toilet paper and other cleaning supplies.

For those who are more proactive and lived through leaner times, we knew there were options. Yes, we ensured we had a large enough supply of toilet paper but also knew there were other products that would serve the purpose.

For example, what happens to a restaurant when they cannot have in house dining? As we learned early in the pandemic, many gave up. Others, however, pivoted to takeout and delivery. Some created virtual chef dinners and wine tastings. They pivoted from where they were instead of panicking and giving up.

Was that a mistake? I don't think so.

Given that within a year, over 500,000 died in the U.S. and over 120 million in the world, caution was warranted. However, panic was not. Some disagreed and refused to wear masks or socially distance unless required by law. They fostered outbreaks and delayed economic recovery, the very thing they feared.

Losing a loved one, a job, or even a favored practice leaves many wondering, "How will I go on?" Notice how that question fosters panic. Notice how it reflects the belief that their internal strengths are not adequate to conquer the external challenge.

Instead of reacting with the eight flawed thinking practices above, communicate these messages. Note: carefully consider the timing of the comments based on the traumatic event. A grieving parent or spouse needs time before hearing these.

- Yes, we are hurting but we will get through this together.
- There are many opportunities. Let's use this to our advantage.

- This doesn't define who we/you are.
- As bad as this may seem, we have many good choices going forward.
- Let's not jump to conclusions.
- We/you are stronger than you feel. Many see that.
- "We will find a way through this."
- "Life will get better."

Since the loss of my son in 2007, I've consoled several grieving parents who ask through the tears,

"When will the pain stop? When will life go back to the way it was?"

Gently, I respond,

"In some ways the pain will always be there. You will always miss them. But you will become stronger. You will find your new normal and learn to live again."

Disruptions change our lives forever, whether we want them to or not. Our choice is to look forward and find the opportunity.

### #2. This will get better.

The world is not going to end with any disaster unless you die. I apologize for the bluntness. Life goes on even if our favorite coffee shop closes. Quarantines end. Schools will resume. The stock market will bounce back. Even in the absolute worst of times, things get better.

Look back to the 2007 recession. It took some time, but the economy recovered and reached record heights.

Look back at the Great Depression. As I've written in the book on my parents, *Humble Homesteaders*, my paternal grandfather did not harvest a crop in three of four years. One year he planted the same crop three times and never got a harvest. How much more difficult can that get?

Look at several great leaders who failed or were labeled as failures.
- Steven Spielberg: rejected twice for entrance into University of Southern California's film school.
- Thomas Edison: A teacher told he him he was "too stupid to learn anything." Took 10,000 times to invent the light bulb.

Walt Disney: A newspaper supervisor told him he had no imagination. A company stole his first cartoon character, Oswald the Rabbit.

Albert Einstein: H didn't start speaking until he was four, reading until he was seven, and was thought to be mentally handicapped. He struggled to get a professorship but wrote his breakthrough work while working as a low-level clerk.

J.K. Rowling: She was a broke, depressed, divorced single mother simultaneously writing a novel, "Harry Potter."

Abraham Lincoln: Failed in business, his sweetheart died, was defeated seven times for various offices before being elected President.

Oprah Winfrey: Fired as a newscaster before landing her own talk show.

Stephen King: His first book, *Carrie*, was rejected by 30 publishers. Dejected, he threw the book into the trash. His wife convinced him to resubmit.

Tom Brady: Was drafted in the 6$^{th}$ round of the NFL draft because he was considered too slow, lacking the stature, strength, arm strength, and throwing ability to play in the NFL.

Michael Jordon: Was cut from his high school basketball team.

Taken from (Lifehack.com)

Everybody suffers a setback at one time or another. The great leaders pivot to do what many think is unlikely or even impossible. They do it by changing the way they think. They don't panic and give up. Instead, they change their pattern of thinking as described in the previous point. They pivot and focus to see the opportunities in their Next Normal.

Communicate this powerful and encouraging message, "This isn't the end. Thing will get better because I will have another opportunity to break through."

## #3. There are incredible opportunities now.

Major disruptions in our lives stop us in our tracks, punch us in the gut, and often land us on our backs. We likely don't realize it at the time but may have been the best thing that ever happened to us.

Don't misunderstand me. I don't wish failure or trauma on anyone. However, Tough Times often wake us up.

Candy Lightner wouldn't have started Mothers Against Drunk Driving and change many laws across the United States had she not lost her daughter to a drunk driver.

No one wants to lose a child, especially to the irresponsible behavior of others. But Lightener chose to find the incredible opportunities embedded in the tragedy.

I have found the same energy. Following my son's suicide, my wife and I made a promise, "His life and death will not be in vain." To that end, I became more impatient with my success. Three years later my wife and I authored *The ROI of Compassion* and have spoken at several conferences on compassionate leadership. Over the years, I have noticed that our bruises become our business, our misery becomes our ministry. Because we have been through the trauma, we are equipped to help others going through it. That means our pain makes things possible that weren't before.

The challenge for Pivotal Leaders is to quickly identify the possibilities and quickly pivot to seize the best of those opportunities.

Communicate this pivotal and disruptive message: "This may be our breakthrough opportunity. "

### #4. You have choices.

Not only do we have great opportunities, but we have choices in how we react. Some react in fear because they don't think they have a choice over their emotions. They believe they can only react. We discussed that in the first point.

Beyond that, followers and managers are focused on the present, not the future. They haven't trained themselves to focus on the future and focus on the potential opportunities. In other words, they haven't learned to track the trends and forecast the best opportunities. It's as if they have been driving by looking out the rearview mirror. All that does is create accidents.

But Next Normal Leaders see a multitude of choices. They quickly separate the good from the bad and then choose to purse the best. They don't just think in an either/or polarity. Life isn't just a choice between good and bad but between good and best. In my first book, *Chevettes to Corvettes: 8 Gears to Leading Your Disruptive Business* fosters the thinking that the enemy of the ultimate is ordinary. Too many settle for good results when they could do much better. Choices come with many options.

Brian May cofounded the rock band Queen and went on to have a stellar career as a singer, songwriter, and record producer. But even as the band was launching, he was busy studying astrophysics. In 2007, he earned his Ph.D.

David Brian also had choices. He was a pre-med student at Rutgers with a 4.0 average. He was a sure bet for medical school when he changed directions to play keyboards and sing with Bon Jovi.

Jeff Bezos had a successful computer science career on Wall Street before starting a small, online book sales company named Amazon.

Julia Child was in marketing and advertising before writing her first cookbook at age 50.

Martha Stewart had a successful modeling career before becoming a Wall Street stockbroker and hosting a gourmet cooking show.

We all have more choices than we might think, especially during Tough Times. You may not be as talented or as financially secure as the list above, but you have more than one choice.

We cannot control the outside events, especially during a trauma or a pandemic, but we can choose to see the positive.

*"You cannot control what happens to you, but you can control your attitude toward what happens to you, and in that, you will be mastering change rather than allowing it to master you."*
Brian Tracy

Communicate this positive and powerful message to your team, "Let's choose to see the positive choices we have at our fingertips."

## #5. Some have it worse and they are surviving.

When bad things happen, we often feel like it couldn't get any worse. But when we stop and look around, we often find that others have it much worse. Sometimes, they are doing much better.

Observation is a powerful tool for Pivotal Leaders. You have already read that the secret is tracking the trends. That demands noticing what is happening. Pivotal Leaders develop a diligent habit and keen focus because they don't want to be surprised. They know their leadership responsibilities require their attention to details inside and outside the organization. They need to notice the trends in the market and the world because they impact the viability of the company. They need to notice the trends inside the company. Trends of performance and productivity dictate profitability.

That habit of observation becomes a strength during Tough Times. That strength comes from understanding the severity of the situation. By looking at others and how they are faring, the Next Normal Leader can accurately assess their situation.

If others are doing worse, there is empathy and a realization that you aren't doing as poorly as you might think. That provides some hope.

If others had it worse and are now doing better, that provides hope.

If others are doing better, there is something to learn from them. That provides hope.

Although our success isn't necessarily dictated other's results, we can be encouraged. It's not that we gleefully celebrate their troubles, but that we understand the situation better.

Communicate this message in a positive way. "If someone else can do that in their situation, maybe it isn't so bad for us."

### #6: This is a great opportunity to make us stronger.

Great teams need tough challenges to show their strength. Use that difficulty to be the challenge to secure your breakthrough. Seeing this as an opportunity for your breakthrough helps you to think bigger and then reach higher.

Lukianoff and Haidt (2018) refer to this principle as "antifragility." It's more than what doesn't kill us makes us stronger. It is that we need the tough times to make us stronger. We need those stressors to help us learn, adapt, and grow. In other words, this is a great opportunity to make us stronger.

> *When we long for life without difficulties, remind us that oaks grow strong in contrary winds and diamonds are made under pressure.*
> Peter Marshall

Communicate this disruptive message to yourself and your team: "This isn't just a difficult situation; this is our opportunity to breakthrough."

**Your Challenge**
Which of these tactics can you apply to become more focused today?

How will becoming focused help you to think bigger and reach higher?

# 3: ENGAGE YOUR TEAM

"We are all in this together."

That slogan became prominent during the COVID pandemic but reflected the 9/11 terrorist attacks and World War II. Trauma creates community where we are all needed to defeat the common foe.

In building that community, Pivotal Leaders must engage their team, showing compassion, and working to alleviate their pain. Without that connection and communication, there will be concern, doubt, and eventually disconnection.

**Compassion and the Workplace**

As we mentioned before, compassion is the best business practice because it unleashes the ultimate performance, production, and profits. If you want to improve the bottom line, you must come alongside your internal and external team members to help alleviate their pain. That will become even more important in the Next Normal, in part, because some leaders are more self-serving.

For example, during the shutdown of 2020, leaders started demanding more of virtual workers. When they should have been enjoying a better work/life balance, workers were pushed to work more hours. Those leaders probably thought, "Great. We have increased productivity."

But have they?

Or have they simply found a new way to inflict pain. Is that smart? Or is it part of their "push them as hard as we can, use them up, and let them go" philosophy?

I discussed that in *Making More Money in Tough Times* as the Manifest Destiny paradigm. Those leaders' rape, pillage, and plunder because they think they have the positional power to do so. But what is the long-term effect?

In our recently renamed book, *Engage Employees*, (previously *Leading with the Power of Compassion*, 2018), we detailed how many of the pains employees report are easily remedied. For example, the 2017 Gallup State of the American Workplace reported that most employees are not given one compliment a week. How easy is that to remedy? How much better will an employee feel when they are praised? How will that improve their performance? How will that increase productivity? How will that boost profits?

Now imagine how that affects businesses during difficult times. We find that companies generate their best ROI when they help employees cope during traumatic times that occur outside of the workplace. The New Normal is inflicting pain on companies around the globe and that is an opportunity for leaders to engage and reap the benefits.

**The Compassion Process**

How can we be more compassionate, helping to alleviate the pain of our employees and customers while ensuring our viability as a business?

My wife and I defined compassion as "coming alongside another to help alleviate their pain." Those organizations and leaders who practice compassion daily unleash the ultimate performance, production, and profits by creating an engaged culture. The leadership principle detailed in *The ROI of Compassion* is simple. "They engage when we engage. They begin to care when we show we care. Their pain is our pain, whether we want it or not."

> *"I've learned that people will forget what you said, people will forget what you did, but people will never forget how you made them feel."*
> Maya Angelo

To engage workers in their pain during a transition to the Next Normal, whether that is a transition through the traumatic or daily

frustrations, my wife and I created a four-step compassion model. This model includes:
1. Noticing,
2. Feeling (from their perspective),
3. Strategically Thinking (how to help alleviate their pain), and
4. Acting (at the appropriate time.)

The first two steps comprise empathy, sensing their pain, that when combined with the last two steps form compassion.

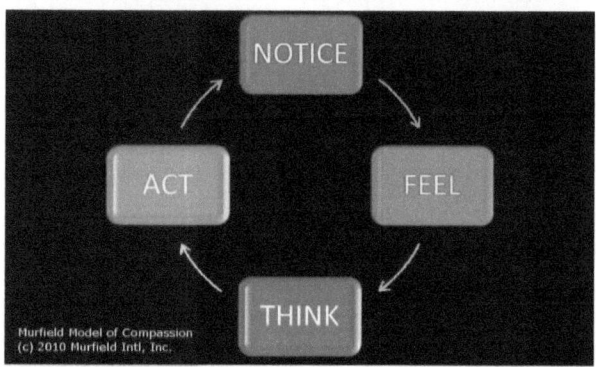

**NOTICE:** As leaders, pay attention to your team. Notice their routine, behavior, communication, and performance. Has it changed? What is their pain?

**FEEL:** Now switch. Looking at the situation from their perspective, why is this situation painful? Don't judge. Everyone has specific needs so you want to see the situation through their eyes, ears, and heart. Listen carefully to appreciate and understand their pain from their perspective.

**THINK:** Now switch back to your perspective. Ask yourself, and other appropriate team members, "How can we best help alleviate their pain?" Create the policy and detail the action plan that will be effective. NOTE: Don't get distracted from your purpose. It is easy to create a policy or take an action that makes us feel good but doesn't alleviate their pain.

**ACT:** Take the action at the appropriate time to help alleviate the pain.

## 8 Needs of Team Members

Employees will face eight different types of challenges during the transition to a New Normal. The transition will bring a wide range of pain depending on the level of trauma. However, if the Pivotal Leader ignores small pains long enough, they become major factors in disengagement. Ignoring traumatic pain will bring disengagement quickly. Also, ignoring the pain of one employee will multiply as others forecast their future with you. As business leaders, especially Human Resources, managers, and executives, we are wise to be mindful that pain causes disengagement.

We also must recognize that facing trauma is not simple. It is often overly complicated and time consuming. Unfortunately, most of us are clumsy when dealing with someone else's pain. We quickly become uncomfortable, not sure what to do, how to feel, or what to say. The silence, however, is deafening for those in any level of pain. It screams "You don't care."

Prevention is worth a pound of cure. Compassion is the secret sauce to engaging employees and building and innovative culture. When you care and show you care during their difficult moment, they usually reciprocate with loyalty. That is why there is such a high return on investment. However, some leaders refuse to believe that compassion is anything more than an unnecessary or ill-advised business expense. They ignore the cost of turnover, presenteeism, and disengagement. They fail to see how small gestures make a big difference. Those gestures, such as stopping to notice how an employee is doing or taking time to listen to their concerns, deliver significant returns over the short and long term.

Claire and her husband dearly wanted children. The moment they received the good news that they were pregnant, they began planning. Together with their families, they equipped and decorated the nursery. With each day, they anticipated their live together with their little bundle of joy. But one day, Claire noticed something wasn't right. Despite the efforts of caring physicians, they suffered a miscarriage. Imagine her pain.
Allow yourself to feel her pain.

Also imagine how she felt as she laid in her hospital bed realizing her hopes and dreams were dashed, at least temporarily and possible permanently. Imagine then how she felt when her manager came to the hospital to see her. Imagine the warmth flooding over her knowing that someone from work went out of their way to show concern. Stumbling to find the right words, she, the manager said, "I'm, uh, sorry to hear what happened."

Imagine the tear that must have come to Claire's eye at the unexpected concern.

The manger continued, "I was just wondering, when will you be able to return to work. I mean, we have that important project, and you are the lead."

Now imagine how Claire felt. Did you feel the frigid wave? Then imagine what Claire told her co-workers. I imagine she it would have gone something like this. "Can you believe that she came to see me only to ask how long before I could drag myself out of a hospital bed and get back to work. She doesn't care about me. You can bet it won't take me long to find a different job with a better boss."

This is a true story and one that is repeated in various versions every day. The manager missed an opportunity to help their team member pivot to their next normal. In the process, she lost a good employee that she relied upon. All it would've taken was a little compassion. That small investment would have yielded great returns. Now imagine how that negatively affected the departmental culture. By noticing how their manager treated Claire, they predicted how they would have been treated. Compassion and the lack of compassion have ripple effects. Helping your team pivot during their painful moments will yield a significant ROI when they gladly help your organization pivot through its painful moment. Failing to care disengages when you need them most. Compassion engages and helps you lead your team, pivoting to the ultimate performance, production, and profits.

This pivot happens when you come alongside your team members in each of eight critical areas: Physical, Emotional, Intellectual, Career, Financial, Family, Social and Spiritual.

**Physical Needs**

We begin with physical needs because that is often the easiest to notice. The pivotal leader engages their team members by noticing any change in their health or physical wellbeing. The pandemic was a direct threat to our physical health and highlighted this area of concern and pain. Notice that in the early stages of the pandemic that we were hyperalert to anyone sneezing or coughing. As we transition out of the pandemic, we still notice but wonder whether it is simply a cold or something worse.

Pivotal leaders engage by caring first about their wellbeing. Don't be like Claire's manager. (By the way, most assume Claire's manager was a man by his insensitivity. That wasn't correct.) Her manager didn't care about Claire except for her ability to complete the project. You will deliver the best ROI when you notice their perspective, not yours. The need for empathy is rarely greater than when one is hurting physically or emotionally.

**Psychological Needs**

Everyone wants to live in a world that is predictable, safe, and comfortable. The uncertainty during times of transition, especially those traumatic moments, violates our predictability, safety, and comfort levels. Trauma strips away our ability to forecast the future. The pandemic left us wondering what the future will look like. Not only did we put our lives on hold for a year, we lost our pattern for living. The old normal was shattered and the new pattern was yet to be defined. We didn't know what life was becoming or how long it would take to be established. The pain of "I don't know" left us uncertain and insecure. We didn't know whether to say we were working from home, working remotely, or working virtually. Suddenly, instead of going our own ways during the day, the entire family was quarantined in a suddenly too small of a home. We quickly pivoted to virtual work and Zoom but felt the pain of loneliness.

One of the best things Pivotal Leaders did during the pandemic was to reach out to each of their team members and ask, "How are you?" They listened carefully beyond just work demands. They listened to their emotional pain.

Listening is a critical component of communication. Actually, I contend that listening is the most important aspect. Communication is the negotiation of shared meaning, not getting our message across. We are all vastly different and unique people. We cannot assume they hear the message the way it is in our heads. Until we take the time to listen for their emotional concerns and appreciate their pain, we cannot speak effectively.

Pivotal leaders listen for psychological pain.

As a leader, communicate with them to help them.

Notice the emotional pain of what is unpredictable. Everyone is different so be careful to understand their unique perspective.

Then feel from their perspective. You may not think it is a big deal. "Suck it up buttercup, get to work" isn't empathetic or helpful in pivoting to the next, best opportunity. Come alongside of them to fully appreciate their pain. Dare to walk in their shoes and feel their pain from their perspective.

Then you can strategize for what will help them pivot best. Compassion is custom fit, not a one size fits all approach. Think through what will help them transition into that next normal where they seize their best opportunities. This follows the same strategic planning process you use at work, only abbreviated. Those in trauma don't need lectures of blame. They don't need to hear how you think they should have done something. Save the "woulda, shoulda, coulda" comments. Instead, structure a plan to address their emotional needs and build them into the mentally strong member of your team.

The last step puts the strategy into action. When dealing with psychological pain, act quickly. Inaction or a delayed reaction is often seen as not caring. Timing is of the essence in dealing with emotional pain. However, an appropriate hug, a few sensitive words, or simply being present with them may speak volumes. Take the action necessary to pivot their world into the as predictable, safe, and comfortable next normal.

**Intellectual Needs**

Trauma leaves us stunned. We don't know what we don't know so how are we supposed to pivot to the next normal?

Thinking back to the beginning of the pandemic, notice that the most pressing need for most employees was the need for information. What are we going to do? Where are we going to do it? How are we going to do it? How long will we need to do it? Sometimes the question was, "Why?" Too often, even the best pivotal leaders didn't have the answers because no one did.

As we discussed previously, reducing uncertainty is critical. Feel their uncertainty and help them determine what information they need most. Remember communication is the process of coming to a shared meaning, which is critical for reducing uncertainty. Act urgently to listen carefully and then provide the necessary information.

Notice in the pandemic, it was critical to ask several questions.
Who is most at risk?
What can be done?
What can I believe?
What can be done to prevent this from happening again?

The pivotal leader communicates the who, what, when, where, how, and even why action is being taken. Team members interpret silence as either a) a hidden agenda of management, b) an insensitivity to their needs, or c) managerial incompetence. When the leader remains silent, followers fear the worst. Say what needs to be done show them what you are doing.

The need for information is only satisfied by providing the information at the earliest point. Saying, "I don't know but will help you find out" is the best response when you don't know.

**Family Needs**

People care about their family. When their family is ill or their needs change, your employees are distracted and cannot deliver peak performance. As a leader, be conscious and compassionate towards these needs. The sooner you can help them address their legitimate needs, the quicker they can help you pivot.

Notice which team members are Caretakers. Know that over 43 million workers care for a family member, most of them over the age of 65 and most vulnerable to this virus. Many are caring for that parent in the employee's home. Others care for the family member by helping them with errands. That parent or family member likely lives in their own residence. Still others live in care facilities. As seen in the Kirkland, Washington nursing home deaths, this population is extremely vulnerable to the disease. (Caregiver.org. and Fox.com)

Notice those with young children in Childcare. (What percentage of your workforce cares for their children? How many are in daycare? How many go to school? Who takes care of those children if the schools or daycare closes?)

Notice how much attention they are giving their own Self-Care. (Caregivers are not only trying to do their own jobs but are responsible for aging relatives. It is taxing enough to avoid being infected for their own good, but they have added responsibilities. Who takes care of their family if they are infected?)

Feel the pain of caretakers. They are good. moral people who care deeply for others. Think how they make your organization valuable. What can you do to help alleviate their pain? As leaders of organizations, our resources have limits. However, there may be outside resources that would help them. Act quickly to share that information and anything else you can do.

Strategize the best action to alleviate their pain. What can you do to adjust your policies to accommodate these caregivers? Do they need flex time, working remotely, or short-term leave? What other ways can you come alongside of your employees to help alleviate their pain.

Lastly, take the action at the best time. That is often asap.

**Career Needs**

Notice that team members need jobs. One of the very real fears of any pivot is the insecurity of employment. The pandemic and 2008 recession brought an accompanying economic downturn. The terrorist attacks of 9/11 sent tremors across the economy. Whatever the pivot, people will be concerned about their jobs.

My wife, Lisa, works as a human resources manager. In 2006, her employer sold the company. She wisely did her research and recognized that the pivot could easily leave her without a job. She knew this was no merger, and even if it were, duplicate jobs would be eliminated. A year later, her suspicions were correct, and her job was eliminated.

Feel the pain of lost wages, either a reduction in hours or loss of their job. Feel the pain of establishing a good rapport with the executive team and then being forced into the job market. Feel the uncertainty of finding a new job that you enjoy. Feel the pain of potentially relocating.

Then think through the options you have to help them pivot. A few years later, after quickly landing an even better job, she was on the other end. The 2008 recession forced her company to lay off a number of people. Remembering her own pain and recognizing theirs, she worked to help each one of them find a new position equal to their own position. How do you think that made them feel? How do you think they talked about their former employer? Instead of a bad review, they would now give a considerate, understanding good referral.

As we exit the pandemic, leaders are confronted with the future of work. Think through the practicalities and urgency of working virtually. Remember the statistics we noted earlier about the vast number of employees that want to work from home at least one or two days a week. They want a job but want a hybrid model. How do you respond? Do you claim this was just a pause and now you are returning to the old normal? Or are you willing to enter into the new, next normal that provides the best of both worlds? That will require thinking through how you will pivot your leadership. Managing and leading in the next normal with a hybrid workplace is not the same as an in-person workforce. A remote workforce will not tolerate expanded hours, expecting that they are always logged on and immediately responding to your whims. This is a major pivot for most in leadership positions. But remember, compassion is the best business strategy and practice because it delivers the ultimate performance, production, and profits.

Think through your policy about Paid Leave. The U.S. Bureau of Labor Statistics reports that Paid sick leave was available to 71 percent of workers in private industry in March 2018. Paid sick leave was available to 31 percent of workers with an average wage in the lowest 10 percent and to 92 percent of workers with an average wage in the highest 10 percent. For those with paid leave, exert your authority for the benefit of the entire team and require infected team members to go home. For those without paid leave, pay them if possible. It will be far less expensive in the long run. Turnover is extremely expensive.

Think through your policies. Are they in writing? Have they been shared and discussed? Did you listen to the potential pain of these policies before constructing them? Is your policy adequate to alleviate employee pain and ensure your viability as a business? If not, create a policy or revise the old one reflects your values, engages your employees, and delivers the best long-term success for the organization.

Act with urgency.

## Financial Needs

Notice the financial cost in a layoff or termination to either your employee or their partner. Understand and appreciate how becoming a caretaker shrinks the family budget, whether it be taking in an aging parent or welcoming a baby. Feel their pain of those additional costs.

Think strategically what you can do to help alleviate them. Granted, it is not the organization's obligation to solve all employee problems. After all, compassion is coming alongside them to help alleviate their pain. Notice the word "help." As we discussed in the *ROI of Compassion*, there is a balance between too little and too much compassion. Insensitivity causes turnover whereas overgenerosity leads to bankruptcy. I know of a college that prided themselves by saying, "We never met an idea we didn't like." Is there any wonder they soon faced financial disaster?

Finding the balance of compassion requires a delicate leadership touch. On one hand, we cannot flippantly make decisions without regard to the financial impact. Yet, we cannot be responsible for their decisions. In between, we can notice and feel for them from their perspective. We can help them by providing in house financial training and connecting them with outside resources.

Act quickly to communicate what can or cannot be done. If assistance can be made, let them know the timeline for the action.

## Social Needs

The pandemic taught us how much we need the social components of the office. We enjoy the spontaneous conversations that foster collegial collaboration. Working remotely doesn't foster that same level of sharing and action.

At the same time, notice that the biggest frustration for most people, beyond the loss of life or health, was separation from their friends and family. We miss being able to hug our parents, children, and grandchildren when socially distancing. We enjoy our favorite extended family.

We also enjoy our social life by dining out, attending parties, and going to concerts. We also enjoy being involved in sporting events and engaging in philanthropic or charitable organizations. These activities bring meaning to our lives. Any type of quarantine restricts those activities and frustrate us.

Feel their pain of isolation that may come from the loss of mobility, health, or a loved one. Also feel the isolation from a downturn in their finances. Remember, allowing yourself to feel from their perspective doesn't mean it is your responsibility to solve the problem. It simply means, at this point in the compassion process, that you feel their pain from their perspective.

Think through what resources you can offer or, probably most appropriate, ones that you can connect them to. Do you have someone in the workplace that knows how to deal with airlines? hotels? event venues? Do you have an in-house attorney? Can you dedicate one or two people to assist with these situations? What can you do to help alleviate their pain?

Some traditional leaders may hesitate or even baulk at the idea that they should be concerned with their employee's social life. But as we detailed in *Leading with the Power of Compassion*, (*Pivotal Engagement*) developing a good friendship at work increases safety and profit. (Gallup 2017.) If that's the case, isn't it a smart move to make their social life, at least at work, a priority in your leadership?

Act. While this situation may not be as urgent as previous ones, it is always critical in showing compassion to do what you say you are going to do at the appropriate time. Keep your promises. This will pay huge dividends in building an engaged and innovative culture.

## Spiritual Needs

Notice that people need a connection to something intangible that helps them make sense of the world. Many practice their religious faiths because it brings immense meaning. Others are more spiritual and less organized in their behavior but still find meaning in a higher being. Still others sense a need for connection but don't outwardly express it. Rest assured that in pivotal times of trauma or uncertainty, everyone turns to something for stability and meaning.

Feel their need for connection and meaning. This is especially true if they have lost a loved one or a job, finances or, have been diagnosed. or are stressed and in a vulnerable status.

Think through this overly sensitive issue. Most workplaces have avoided elements of faith, fearing dissension. This isn't the time to preach to anyone but listen carefully and strategize how you can help them connect in the best way. One of the best ways to approach them is to ask their closest co-workers. They already have the trust of that individual and can broach the subject appropriately. Work within their values to help them connect with what they find most beneficial.

Act appropriately in gesture and action. If done well, they will be eternally grateful. If not done well, they will feel violated. Most of all, remember that failing to take any action will be interpreted as not caring. Remember, apathy ruins relationships.

Pivoting to the next normal will work best when you engage your team by exploring each of these areas without being intrusive. When you do, you will seize opportunities that you couldn't have before.

When you are sensitive to each of these eight areas of need, you will engage your team and can begin building an innovative culture.

**Your Challenge**

This may sound like an impossible challenge.

Choose one of your closest team members.

Identify each one of their needs. Be careful to identify their needs according to all 8 categories.

Then complete the needs assessment for each of your team members.

While this may sound overwhelming, once you understand your team this well, you will quickly engage them with what matters most to them.

*"Culture is the formal and informal practices that mark an organizations' character, such as rites and rituals and the display of meaningful artifacts like architecture, interior design, posters, and furniture. Moreover, the cultural approach foregrounds the human desire to organizational life as an opportunity to do something meaningful.*
*(Gendron, 1999).*

# 4: FOSTER AN INNOVATIVE CULTURE

We can no longer live looking back on our past success. To maximize our opportunities in the next normal we need to build engaged teams that are constantly looking for the best opportunities. That requires fostering a cutting-edge culture.

Have you wondered why some organizations are so innovative while others not? May you have wondered how you foster a cutting-edge culture from your leadership position?

In this chapter we examine how organizational culture is critical to innovative organizations. Specifically, we detail seven essential elements and assess how you and your organization fare.

**What is Organizational Culture?**

Simply stated, organizational culture is how you get things done. It starts at the top. If it is your company or department, you set the tone with your "vision, values, norms, systems, symbols, language, assumptions, beliefs, and habits (Cancialosi 2017)

**Who Shapes Your Innovative Culture?**

Executives shape organizations the most. They have the position power to decide and enact the policies. It is their vision of innovation that will drive the team. Beyond the top-level executives, two other groups have the power to shape an innovative culture. However, make no mistake, without the executives fostering an innovative culture, it probably is not going to happen.

## PIVOTAL LEADERS

Departmental leaders shape the atmosphere of their teams. They embrace the vision of the executives but have considerable freedom to set the tone in their departments. Those seeking innovation set a much different tone than those seeking compliance. The elements discussed below illustrate the differences.

The last category is "Everyone Else." Anyone wan work to create an innovative atmosphere. Does that sound misguided? It may but hear me out. We all chose our mindset. Yes, the atmosphere around us does make a difference, but ultimately, we control our own mindset. Our leaders often value thinking creatively to solve significant problems (or even those small and annoying problems.) We can choose to be the problem solver without overstepping our authority.

Many dismiss innovative opportunities because they think they don't have the authority. However, those that welcome a chance to solve problems without stepping on the toes of supervisors or peers will likely be appreciated. If not, they need to look for another place to work or a different way to approach the team leader.

### 7 Elements of Innovative Organizational Cultures

Those seeking to pivot and innovate have a different perspective, foster a different vision, and set a much different atmosphere than those who are merely trying to keep up or survive. Looking at each of the items listed by Needle (2004), let's briefly look at each.

# *PIVOTAL LEADERS*

1. Innovative Vision

First, innovative organizations have a vision of doing what has never been done before. They see a new world and are compelled to make that vision a reality.
- What is your vision?
- In what way does it foster innovation?
- How passionate are you about innovating?

2. Collaborative Values

Second, innovative organizations value radical change. Innovative leaders understand they cannot do it by themselves, so they value collaboration over competition. They also appreciate creative individuals who can make that vision a reality.
- What do you value most?
- How much do you value innovation?
- If you asked the five people who know you best at work, what would they say you value most?

3. Innovative Practices

Third, innovative organizations understand what practices need to be in place to best foster innovation. Maybe the most important note to make here is that they know what rules to ignore. Examine an innovative culture, and you will find that innovative organizations have very few rules because they understand creative individuals needs the freedom to work "outside the box" and to redesign the box.
- How many rules do you require at work?
- What happens when someone does not follow the rules?
- How much energy do you spend to ensure your team follows the rules?
- What does your team think of the rules?

4. Supportive Systems

Fourth, they build systems based on the previous three elements, not some top-down or outside-in synthetic mandate. All organizations find systems that work for them. However, as you will see below, innovative organizations foster flexibility in their systems.
- What systems work best for you?

- When is the last time you assessed the effectiveness of those systems?
- Do they foster more innovation or obedience?

5. Communication

Fifth, Needle uses the terms symbols and language. Those who have studied communication define communication as the symbols and language we use to negotiate shared meaning. Innovative communication is more than just "getting our message across" because we are delving into what others have not experienced. Therefore, innovative communication is using symbols and language to help shape a common understanding among those within the organization as well as vendors, customers, and potential customers.
- What is your style of communication?
- Do you do more speaking than listening? (Be honest.)
- How effective are you in creating shared meaning with your team?

6. Beliefs

Sixth, innovative organizations believe that doing the "impossible" is their mission. Nothing innovative happens if the people working to innovate don't believe it is possible. Disbelief is deadly. Meanwhile, those that believe anything is possible innovate.
- To what degree do you believe you can innovate? (again, be honest)
- Does your team believe the innovation you desire is possible? Why?
- What will it take to build your team's confidence?

7. Habits

Seventh, disruption is a healthy habit innovators hone. A healthy habit is an unconscious behavior that has been purposely developed to ensure the best opportunity to succeed. At the same time, bad habits develop with lazy motivation. Sometimes bad habits were once best practices that are outdated. The innovation habit is challenging to hone because it requires tolerance for failure. Innovation is challenging; playing it safe is often easier. However, those that are innovative have developed a habitual mindset of thinking beyond the failures.

- Do you foster more of an attitude of innovation or playing it safe?
- What is your habit of responding to a failure? Do you immediately cringe or welcome the opportunity to adjust?
- What are the thinking habits of your team?

Notice what actions you take when you have misplaced your keys. Notice how you tend to go back and look in the same place over and over. Normally, those actions don't solve the problem. It isn't until you stop and think that you remember where you set them down.

## Pain

Now notice the pain that persists in the COVID 19 shutdown. Some are laid off and suffering the economic pain. Others are overworked medical professionals and suffering physical pain of exhaustion. Many are suffering the psychological pain, worried they will contract COVID 19. Some are suffering the family pain from losing someone they loved.

Overcoming any of these pains requires that we think bigger, reach higher, and do what seems impossible.

- Disengaged Employees.
- Failing to Anticipate Disruptive Trends.
- Working Through Employee Trauma.
- Minimizing Poor Communication.
- Leveraging the Unique Value of Business and Individuals

## The Problem – Their Pain

The five problems listed above all come down to five key situations.

First, someone is in pain and second, someone needs compassion to resolve their pain.

Disengaged and distracted employees are hurting, and that disengagement hurts the business by damaging performance, production, and profits. Currently, productivity is already suffering by working from home, other family members working from home, and children home from school. Leaders may want to blame it on lazy workers but, when we express compassion by noticing their pain, feeling for them from their perspective, thinking of ways we can help alleviate that pain and then taking that action, we may just find the solution.

Second, we are in a temporary transition to the New Normal.

We didn't see this coming and were not prepared. Failing to anticipate disruptive trends leaves many looking for jobs without the skills or mindset to step into good jobs. Some give up too easily and claim we need another stimulus or even guaranteed national income. The challenge of that pivot may be overwhelming for many. Within that trend, many will struggle to adjust. Compassion, especially noticing and feeling their pain, is critical for maintaining and building success in the New Normal.

Third, the COVID 19 shutdown has traumatized many employees, managers, and business owners.

Trauma is extreme pain that knocks us to our knees and onto our back. We are stunned and temporarily paralyzed. We don't know how to proceed. We may not know if we want to go on. Without compassion, life is incredibly difficult. As we have heard on the commercials, we are in this together. The entire world is affected. To get through, we must think differently than we did before.

Fourth, poor communication costs billions of dollars every year when someone doesn't do what the other person thought they said.

Communication issues are exasperated during COVID 19 when most everyone is working remotely. Compassionate communication focuses on listening and willingness to understand the other person's perspective.

Fifth, even before COVID 19 shutdown, 70% of workers were disengaged.

Why? One reason is that leaders don't fully appreciate the unique value of each team member. Is there any wonder why most workers don't appreciate their own unique value? Dig deeper and can find that many if not most small businesses don't appreciate why they are uniquely valuable to their customers. Then mix in the layoffs and business closings. Many do not know how they are valuable outside of their assigned duties. This is a time to discover our unique value. That takes compassion, not competition.

*"We cannot solve our problems with the same thinking we used when we created them."*
Thomas Edison

From a business perspective, when leaders care to notice the pain, they find opportunities to unleash the ultimate performance, production, and profits. That is why my coauthor and I argue that compassion is the best business strategy and practice.

We agree with Thomas Edison. We need to change our thinking to make a successful transition to the New Normal.

## Innovative Thinking

Unfortunately, COVID 19 and the post pandemic era will change our world whether we like it or not. These "economic earthquakes" will reduce some businesses to rubble. It will change the way we do business and how we live. We won't simply reopen the economy but need to reinvent it. The New Normal began with a sudden shock, a quake followed by many aftershocks of losing beloved stores, restaurants, and habits. At this point, we don't know when the quakes will end. But we do know the New Normal will be drastically different from the past.

The New Normal will see an increase in virtual work, a decrease in the need for commercial real estate, fewer large, live events (at least in the remainder of 2021), and more cautious interactions. Some have even speculated that the handshake may be eliminated forever. Adjusting to that New Normal, especially for business, will be a challenge that is met with innovative thinking. We must think bigger and reach higher to make that transition into the New Normal.

Unfortunately, most of us have not changed our pattern of thinking since high school or in our mid 20's when we finished college and started to find our way in the world. Without the habit of pivoting, our thinking becomes entrenched, reinforcing what we have determined is the right and best way of resolving a problem. We generally fail to keep an open mind to new ideas and new ways of solving problems.

Before you become too puffed-up thinking that is someone else's problem, stop and consider how willing you are to consider alternative methods. Ask yourself, why do you still struggle with persistent problem?

**Think Again**

Adam Grant expresses this concept in his latest book, Think Again (2021). Too often we play the role of preacher, prosecutor, or politician instead of the scientist. As a preacher, we adhere to our sacred beliefs and fail to pivot. The prosecutor only focuses on the pointing out the flaws in the reasoning of others. Then there is the politician whose only goal is to persuade an audience. Meanwhile, the scientist pivots their thinking in a continual search for truth. The scientists are willing to be wrong if new evidence is presented.

Notice the rigidity in the preacher, unwilling to reconsider sacred values. Also notice the mindset of the prosecutor, rigid in their efforts to prove another wrong. Once committed, like the preacher, they are as persistent as a puppy on a pantleg. Then there is the politician. We wonder why they are so ineffective. We need to look no farther than their rigid goal to persuade whoever is in front of them. Always seeking the popular vote, one could say they are willing to pivot to follow the latest trend. But notice they rarely stray from their relentless quest to be re-elected.

**Stretching our Thinking**

Innovation demands breaking from the habitual mindset to create products and services that make our world better, faster, cheaper, and easier. Adam Grant is right, we need to break the habit of our rigid thinking.

Notice what happens when material loses its flexibility. It breaks easily.

Plastic dries out and shatters.

Rubber cracks and leaks.

Leather cracks and deteriorates.

Now look at what happens in the body.

Muscles that are strengthened but not stretched tear, cause pain, and leave us immobile. Like great athletes, we are wise to build the habit of stretching.

I have been using a medical massage therapist since I started running a decade ago. At first, I only went to him to alleviate a pain. Soon I learned that daily stretching reduced the times I needed to see him. It also helped my performance and comfort. It also makes it easier to sit at my desk and write for hours. Strengthen the muscles is necessary but so is stretching them.

In the same way, in my academic studies, I found favorite theorists and authors. It would have been easy and convenient to build my platform and stand on it, defending it from any criticism. However, as Adam Grant writes, that's not the way of a seasoned academic researcher. I'm always willing to hear what and how others think. Why? Because it stretches my mind and perspective to see what I cannot from my current view. Intellectually, I need to be continually stretching to find my best opportunities. Like stretching for running, intellectual stretching prevents being outdated and irrelevant.

Yet I continually see others my age who have slipped into the "I'm old" mentality which means "I'm set in my ways." They are tired of changing and have jumped off the train. Comfortable in their spectator seat to the side of the action, they watch the world go by, too often criticizing that it isn't the way it used to be.

Is that the way you want to live?

Or would you rather be forever young, seeking the new opportunities that make your life better, faster, cheaper, and easier? Yes, it is easier to get old because that takes no effort. It is passive. But who wants to be old? Wouldn't we all rather live in our prime?

**Innovative Thinking**

It all comes down to purposely pivoting our thinking. Constantly look for the better way to do whatever you are doing. Notice the pain. Feel how good it will be when that pain is alleviated. Strategize how you can make that happen. Then, as Nike says, "Just Do It!"

**Your Challenge**

On a scale of 1 to 10 with 10 being the most innovative and 1 being the most repetitive, how open are you to new methods when attempting to solve a persistent problem?

Extremely Repetitive 1 2 3 4 5 6 7 8 9 10 Most Innovative

The only question is, "Will you be part of the rubble or part of the new construction?"

# 5: FIND YOUR UNIQUE VALUE

*"Everyone has a purpose in life and a unique talent to give to others. And when we blend this unique talent with service to others, we experience the ecstasy and exultation of own spirit, which is the ultimate goal of all goals.*
Kallam Anji Reddy

What is your unique value as a leader? What does each of your team members provide that make them uniquely valuable.

**Pivotal Principle #5: Find Your Unique Value**

**Your Prize Inside**

Most individuals work outside-in thinking the world is right-side up. No wonder they are upside down. They fail to fully grasp their unique value and miss incredible opportunities because they did not realize their ultimate value. Most everyone identifies their talents but fail to fully appreciate their uniqueness and ultimate value to customers, employers, and the community.

Whenever I'm in a business meeting with other professionals, I'm listening for what makes them uniquely valuable. Often during introductions, both private and public presentations, someone is introduced with their business title and what service they provide.

That leaves me a bit frustrated. Why?

It is great knowing what they do but I want to know what separates them from all their competitors.

Some do that in their elevator pitch or marketing slogan. But can't we think bigger? Isn't there something even more valuable?

**The Problem of Competition**

Many don't see their unique value. They only know the job they do and the title they are given. That is a serious problem because they have competitors that do the same thing.

They don't know the unique value they offer. Therefore, they don't know how they stand out, why they are so valuable, or why someone who pay top dollar for their service. Maybe the biggest problem is that they do NOT stand out. They are no better than any of the competitors.

No wonder they view the world of business as Kim and Mauborgne described in their book, *Blue Ocean Strategy* (2005). They insist upon swimming where everyone else is swimming. That is where the competition for space and success becomes a blood sport. They fight to the death and believe that is the way of the world. But by swimming farther out, creating products and services that are better, faster, cheaper, and easier, we lose the competition. Phrased that way, why would we want to swim in the bloody, red waters when we can enjoy the blue oceans of opportunity.

**Think Bigger**

My recent book, *The Prize Inside* (2019) is fictitious story of a little boy who dared to dream beyond his doubts. He struggles to find his unique value, especially living in his older brother's shadow. To move beyond those debilitating doubts and step into his limelight, he had to pivot his thinking.

Many of us can relate. We are so accustomed to living the life and running the business the way others tell us that we have not discovered or have forgotten what makes us uniquely human and valuable. Corporate business in their highly structured, repeatable processes often strip our uniqueness away. Employees with names are relegated to "talent" or positions.

Look at the way corporate works. People are depersonalized to fit into the old Theory X management model. Serving as easily replaceable cogs in the corporate machine, their uniqueness is chipped away and discarded. Uniformity is prioritized over uniqueness.

This is seen in a call center. The employees were governed by rigid rules for performance. True to the Theory X model, everything is measured and monitored to increase efficiency, productivity, and profitability. One particular call center depersonalized the process to such an extent that employees were only allowed on photo in their cubicle. In many ways, employees were no more than an easily replaced cog. Is there any wonder they had such a high turnover?

While that might have been understandable in the old industrial paradigm of doing business, it doesn't work in the digital age of transparency, authenticity, and worldwide competition. With an ever-increasing tendency, customers want to identify with a business that shares their values. How can they do that if you don't know your unique value?

**My Way or the Highway**

A friend, Alinda, that built a good book of business as an employment recruiter at XYZ Recruiting. Her job was to secure businesses that would use her employer's agency to fill their needs for office help. In her 40s, she was confident, successful, and very personable, consistently leading the company in sales.

In a pivot for the company, the new owner, John, took over and immediately imposed his leadership philosophy that was only concerned about profits, not clients or staff. Over the first two weeks, he fired several that didn't conform exactly as he demanded. He demanded a "butts in seats" model and openly told his staff they were "minions."

Nice guy, huh? To be fair, business must focus on the bottom line. He was the owner and can manage how he pleases. However, as the leader, he must also take the responsibility for his actions.

He quickly fired the outside sale person and put Alinda in that position. In a twist she didn't expect, instead of visiting clients she was expected to call them from her desk. John reasoned that she could do more work and get more results that way.

However, Alinda knew that her unique value came in building relationships, not just making sales. She understood that businesses could choose from a number of recruiting agencies but would do business with those they knew best, liked, and trusted. So, she built great relationships and became known for being a person of integrity. Stated simply, they trusted her, and she delivered.

But that didn't fit John's philosophy and he was not going to bend to fit her model. Afterall, this was his business. It was his way or the highway. If she didn't like it, she could leave.

Think about that. John failed to see what made her successful. He didn't appreciate why his clients used his services instead of choosing a competitor. Even when she tried to explain, he wouldn't hear or understand that her rapport with customers came from the in-person visits. Instead, he inflicted his model on his best employee. Is there any wonder she went looking and soon landed a better job? Also, is it any surprise that company sales quickly plummeted. Also, isn't it predictable that he would try to use a mutual friend to rehire her. Of course, he wouldn't humble himself and apologize.

In his ignorance (or stupidity) he refused to see or appreciate her unique value. He was blinded from seeing that sales and profit came because of her unique value, not the name of his company. Without her they were just another placement office. Without Alinda, clients had no loyalty to XYZ Recruiting.

**What Can I do?**

I was a college communication studies professor for approximately 15 years. At one point, I served as the department chair and advised 35 students plus teaching four classes per semester. I chose communication as a major as an undergraduate because I valued the process. Returning to college at age 31, I loved learning how to speak in public, debate important issues, and solve problems in small groups. But it was more than just learning skills. As I entered graduate work, I dug deeper and appreciated the process of thinking involved in negotiating shared meaning (communicating.) I explored the emotional power of language to either create or destroy. I soon learned to deconstruct stories and uncover hidden meanings.

My goal was to pass this perspective and knowledge on to others earning their college degrees. That led me to becoming a professor. Notice that I was looking for a position at a college. The hiring process looks to find a good fit between candidate and college. Hiring is like becoming engaged and tenure is similar to a marriage, building a long-term relationship that is mutually beneficial and collaborative.

Part of my job at my second professorship involved serving as department chair and advisor to 35 students. Having worked factory and warehouse jobs for a decade, I passionately wanted to help them avoid the mistakes I made and find the niche in the world. I began my advising sessions each semester with one question.

"What do you want to be doing in 5 years?"

Almost every student answered with the same answer.

"I don't know."

Part of their confusion came from a misguided perspective entering college. Too many assume college prepares students for a job. While some majors do have a vocational focus such as engineering, nursing, or teaching, many do not. This is particularly true in the liberal arts, which communication studies normally is found. The liberal arts are uniquely valuable for helping us understand who we are and who we can become. In many ways, it helps us find our unique value. Unfortunately, the vocational advocates only see the two-dimensional perspective of "get a job." Their goal is get a job and make money. The focus on what can I "do" to make money. They are not concerned about "who I am and who am I becoming?"

At the same time, the liberal arts also become two-dimensional, sacrificing the third dimension of "getting a job." No wonder they are limited to tending bar or other types of service and sales.

Understanding the need for all three dimensions. They need a good general education with a major, minor and electives. Their general education requirements bring a breadth that they won't find without a college degree. I knew because I had been there. But then I surprised them.

"You are majoring in communication studies. Minor in business and take elective courses in psychology."

"Why?"

"With a minor in business, you will have a trade. That is where you can get a variety of jobs ranging from management to marketing. Psychology will help you understand why people act the way they do. You will understand their motivations better. Then with your major in communication, you will be able to effectively communicate with executives, peers, front line personnel, vendors, customers, and the general public."

Notice that each of the three dimensions are what employers desire. They need applicants to perform a certain job. But to do more than just the entry level job, they need someone who can relate well to others. Implied is a willingness to learn and grow.

## PIVOTAL LEADERS

**Your Prize Inside**

I wished I would have written *The Prize Inside* and *Conversations with My Future Self* to have shared it with my students. That was the missing piece to their education. Too many chose communication and other liberal arts because they loved art or music or communication. Too many others chose the major because they didn't know what else to do. That is the secret is to find what makes each of us uniquely valuable.

Identifying our prize inside is the first step. Second, we must value that prize inside, understanding how we uniquely benefit others. Third, we develop the knowledge, skills, and attitude to own that prize inside. Fourth, we are then challenged to share our prize with those that will appreciate it. That is a glaring problem for many, in part because many organizations don't care about what makes their employees uniquely valuable. Instead, they focus only on production and their organizational policies, much like Alinda's new owner. Lastly, when we find that fit, the organization celebrates us for who we are at our best. That is when we can celebrate ourselves and enjoy the best opportunities.

Once we can celebrate our prize inside and have others celebrating it, we can pivot quickly, looking for the best opportunities for us. We are not swimming in the bloody waters of competition as much as we are finding blue oceans of great opportunities.

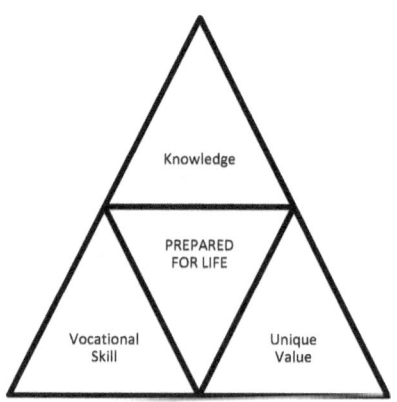

## Your Team's Prize Inside

We need to return to the fourth stage of sharing our prize inside. As pivotal leaders, we know who we are and the unique value we provide. However, that is only part of the formula to pivot our organizations. We need to help others pivot. To that end, our charge is to help others find their unique value beyond their job description. Pivot from simply looking for or developing a specific skill to tapping their passion for a certain body of knowledge. Help them fine tune their attitude to welcome change, improvement, and success.

Unfortunately, too often managers are the obstacles to pivoting. They focus so much on maintaining that they squelch new growth. Some, maybe most, make their employees one dimensional. Like the call center, they are not concerned about what brings meaning to that employee. No wonder they are disengaged. That sterile, work only focus creates a pain. Then consider the disengagement discussed in the Gallup 2017 State of the Workplace. The mast majority of managers fail to give one compliment a week to team members. Hidden within that report is a cry for celebrating each member's unique value. Without that celebration, doubt, skepticism, and disengagement grow. The ability to quickly pivot is diminished if not lost entirely.

## Your Challenge

You can begin to sense your value with the following 3 questions.

1. What specific problem do you help others solve?
2. How do you solve the problem better, faster, or cheaper than your competitors or co-workers?
3. Why do your loyal customers keep coming back? (Why does your boss continue to employ you?)

# 6: CHALLENGE YOUR TEAM

Pivotal Leadership shifts to see the great opportunities.

Even though we are only on the sixth principle, I challenge you to do something in the next 21 days that will significantly change your life. That's right. Let's use the current situation to be disruptive right now.

**The Value of a Challenge**

Before I give you the challenge, let's examine the value of a challenge. A challenge poses an opportunity to test your skill, improve your game, and achieve a higher level. You know that a challenge is critical to high performance teams, keeping them sharp and consistently at the cutting-edge.

Challenge is also important for life. Unfortunately, as we have discussed, too many favor comfort over challenge. They are impatient for a time where they are not challenged. They can't wait to retire or at least find an easier position.

That creates a significant problem according to neuroscientist and author of *Successful Aging (2020)*, Daniel Levitin. Most everyone would like to avoid aging. I doubt anyone wants to develop Alzheimer's or any type of dementia. What keeps us alive, and sharper longer is the challenge to keep our brains active. Stopping, i.e., retiring in the classic sense of sitting in a rocking chair and passing the day, is the worst thing we can do. We are wise to follow musician Judy Collin's advice, "Never

Stop. That's the key. Never Stop. Never stop growing. Never stop thinking that there's something you want to do that you haven't done. And do it!" No wonder she is still traveling, performing, and writing in her eighties.

> *"Never Stop. That's the key. Never Stop. Never stop growing. Never stop thinking that there's something you want to do that you haven't done. And do it!"*
> Judy Collins

Jane Goodall, well into her 80s, is still researching the social and family interactions of chimpanzees in her Tanzania center. She says, "People who retire fade rather fast unless they have something really important to do. It's feeling that you have purpose, and that you have less and less time to make your mark. Instead of slowing down, you have to speed up." (in Levitin, p. 135).

Our challenge is to not slow down at any point, even during trauma. We keep moving ahead, learning, and growing when we accept the challenge.

Pivoting is critical at all stages of life. Those willing to be Pivotal Leaders, can never stop learning and growing. Unfortunately, 27% of Americans didn't read a book last year. It's not that they didn't read a book completely, they didn't read one at all. (Perrin, 2019) Worse yet, "43% of high school graduates never read another book the rest of their lives and 42% of college grads never read another book after college. 70% of US adults have not been in a bookstore in the last five years and 80% of US families did not buy or read a book last year." (Granger, 2019).

In a recent conversation with a former television news producer, when I suggested one of my books, she quickly replied, "I don't read books over 100 pages." I've heard from other authors that they have begun writing shorter books because readers won't accept the challenge of a longer book.

Yet, popular authors like Adam Grant, Simon Sinek, thrive with longer books. Might the real reason be that fewer people are willing to challenge themselves?

In this chapter I challenge you to push beyond your current perspective. Following the mindset of Jane Goodall, I challenge you to speed up and find renewed purpose with a business and then personal challenge.

**Your Business Challenge**

Choose one of the items on the list below or do something else. All that matters is that it is something that makes your life (and those around you) that you have not done before. Below are several ways you can make more money from your business, expand your products, or serve in a different way.

1. Start a blog.
2. Write a new blog post series about a topic you haven't covered before,
3. Start a newsletter.
4. Open a new market.
5. Create a new product.
6. Create a new service.
7. Write a new book.
8. Write a completely different type of book.
9. Learn a new business skill.
10. Change business paradigms.
11. Read a new business book.
12. Take a business-related course.
13. Write and launch a business course.
14. Create a fee-split partnership.
15. Collaborate on a new business venture.
16. Encourage an employee.
17. Hold a meeting with your executive team simply to listen to their ideas, concerns, and perspective.
18. Purposely pause to engage the person perceived as the lowest ranking employee.
19. Ask you employees to identify their biggest work frustration.
20. Ask all employees for suggestions to your biggest problem.
21. Make a movie about your work culture.
22. After a worker has gone home, go sit at their workstation to see their world from their perspective.
23. Go visit your most challenging customer. Listen to their concerns.

24. Celebrate an employee who is rarely celebrated.
25. Write your own termination letter. Detail why it would be warranted. Don't claim "that would never happen." Project that it did and why. Then work to overcome those challenges.

**Your Personal Challenge**

Now dig deeper and challenge yourself on a personal level. Choose one of the items on the list below or create one of your own. It doesn't matter as much what you choose and challenging yourself. Do make it significant because anything easy isn't really a challenge.

1. Take up a new hobby.
2. Read an old, favorite book.
3. Read a new book.
4. Write a short story.
5. Write a short book.
6. Record your story.
7. Write a screenplay.
8. Make a short movie.
9. Learn a new software.
10. Cook a new recipe.
11. Help someone every day.
12. Connect with one old friend per day.
13. Exercise 30 minutes every day
14. Learn a new song.
15. Study a new topic.
16. Learn a new dance.
17. Play a new instrument.
18. Paint a portrait.
19. Learn a language.
20. Study a new subject (like art history, cultural movements, etc.)
21. Accept another challenge.

Remember, the purpose of a challenge is to push you forward when you feel like quitting. Challenge yourself to do start, continue, revive, or finish a project.

# 7: COMMUNICATE

Too often people see communication as "getting your message across." They think speaking is communication. Change that thought. As we move into the Next Normal, it is time to pivot that word, change the meaning, allow it to transform your leadership.

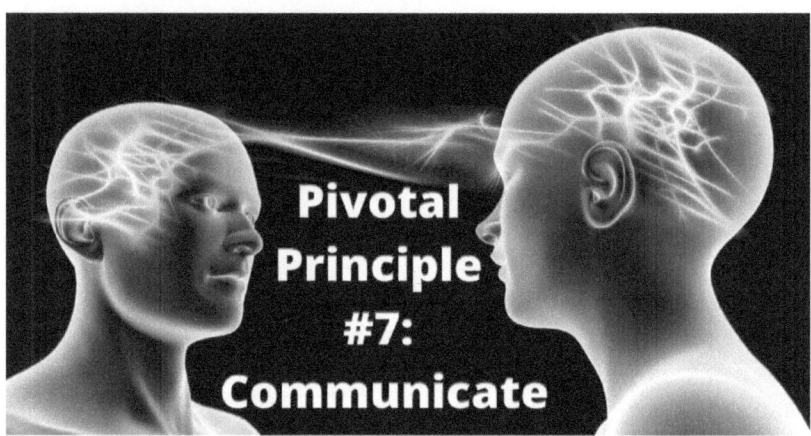

Communication is negotiating a shared meaning between two vastly different people. To effectively negotiate a shared meaning, we listen far more than we speak. We listen compassionately, to identify their pain, feeling with them from their perspective, before strategically thinking through the solution. It is only then that we speak other than to clarify or understand.

Communicating in the Next Normal requires focusing on and alleviating the pain of others. What do they need that they do not have? What do they want that has been taken from them? What have they been charged to do but they don't have the resources to finish? Leaders at every level are most successful when they use compassion as the central point of their leadership communication.

This is a pivot from the physical speaking model.

**The Pain of Uncertainty**

Any shift, espccially a disruptive trauma, causes uncertainty. People look to their leaders to alleviate that uncertainty. The question we must ask ourselves as Pivotal Leaders is, "How can I reduce the uncertainty. How can I instill hope and confidence in team, organization, and community?"

## Uncertainty

Those fears are very real but dig deeper and we find that one of the biggest problems we face is uncertainty. We don't know what will happen. That uncertainty amplifies the fears and causes many more problems, leaving some of the verge of panic.

Panic solves nothing.

So, what do we do?

We stop and notice. There are four critical areas of uncertainty that we face with this epidemic: Physical, Financial, Family, and Social. For example, during the pandemic, employees had the following questions that reflected their uncertainty.

For example, notice the questions we asked during the pandemic for each of these areas.

Physical:
- Will I catch the virus?
- What symptoms will I have?
- Will I die?
- Will I be quarantined?
- If so, for how long?

Family
- Will my family catch it?
- What symptoms will they get?
- Will any of them die?
- Will they need to be quarantined?
- If so, what will I be able to do?

Career
- Will I be able to work from home?
- Will I get paid if I'm out?
- Will the economy tank?
- If so, will I still have a job when it is over?

Financial
- If I don't get paid, how will I pay my bills?

You can ask similar questions in any disruption or trauma.

Physical:
- What concerns do you have about your physical safety?
- What symptoms are you experiencing?
- Is your life in danger?
- If not, what will be the consequences?
- What can I expect from my body in the future?

Family
- How will this affect my family?
- How safe are they?
- How can I protect them?
- How can I best help them?
- What resources are available?

Career
- Is my job at risk?
- What is the future of my industry?
- What will happen to my career?
- What is the job market like?
- What else can I do?
- How will I make a living?

Financial
- If I don't get paid, how will I pay my bills?
- How will I feed my family?
- How will I survive?

**Providing Certainty**

Leading with compassion means coming alongside our team to help them alleviate their pain. In this case, that means feeling their pain and then communicating to reduce their uncertainty.

## PIVOTAL LEADERS

Even a year after the 2020 outbreak, we still don't have all the answers and cannot foretell the future. The same holds for a personal trauma, Even years later, we often don't have all the answers. Corporate buyouts often don't provide certainty of employment for months or years. Whatever the situation, leaders still have tremendous opportunities to help alleviate the pain of employees, customers, vendors, and business associates. The assistance comes by sharing what we know and the action we will take. We can assure them of our values and commitment.

Failing to communicate in a crisis leaves leaders looking like they don't care. Below are 7 ways you can reduce their uncertainty by showing compassion.

1. Meet with your executive team and listen to their concerns. Revisit your core values. Ask your team, "Are these the values we will stand on during this crisis?"

2. Construct compassionate policies. Build the wisest policy concerning attendance, illness, treatment, work responsibilities, pay, etc. Remember, what you do or fail to do during this time will tell employees and customers what you really think of them. Are they trusted team members that you value and will work to save? Or are they expendable in the face of profits?

3. Track the needs of your entire team from executives to front line staff to customers, vendors, and the community.

4. Hold an all-hands meeting. Listen to their concerns. Share what you know and what you will do. Be careful to address each of the four aspects of their uncertainty plus an additional one they voice.

5. Send out an email detailing your action plan.

6. Mode your policy. Be seen doing what you say. One of the biggest concerns is unsanitary surfaces. Since we cannot see germs, have your cleaners visibly cleaning frequently. Wash your hands frequently. Keep your distance. Do all that the CDC recommends.

7. Reassure your team of your commitment to them. Compassion is caring for others. We know

others care when they tell us they care but even more, when they show they care. This is a time where we do both, show it and say it. (Unless you have no commitment to them. If that is the case, we need to have a conversation to show you that compassion is the best business practice with the highest ROI.)

Communicating to create a cutting-edge culture that yields disruptive innovation may be the biggest challenge you face as a leader. In this post, we detail three critical elements that may be the key to your success.

**Shift Paradigms**

Those who follow me are aware that I've studied communication at the Bachelors', Masters and Ph.D. levels. To me, communication is the negotiation of shared meaning, not just "getting my message across." Communication is a dynamic process between two quite different people working to find common ground amidst a world of differences. At its core, communication is a collaborative venture in an extremely competitive world.

No wonder there are so many misunderstandings and conflicts.

Communicating innovation requires the Pivotal Leader to cross that divide and help the team shift paradigms. Together, they are going to do something that is well beyond the norm. Some might even consider it "crazy good." They are going to do what others consider "impossible."

That won't be easy but it is within their grasp if they connect, communicate, and collaborate.

**Speaking: Disruptive Story Telling**

The disruptive leader has a lofty vision. That vision is often so lofty that many followers initially think it is crazy, insane or simply not smart.

Who dares tell that story? Who dares to have such lofty dreams and then is willing to share that "insanity" with others? To make matters even more challenging, who is crazy enough to think that ordinary followers will think they can play a significant part in disruptive innovation?

Disruptive leaders tell crazy stories about what their team will do. It has a vision of crazy results and crazy expectations. Crazy as it is defined on dictionary.com, is something that doesn't make sense to the point of being insane.

Disruption will appear crazy, insane, and totally irrational.

After all, who does these things? Who dares to leave the comfort of "civilization" to live in the wilderness? The disruptive leader does. So do those willing to follow that leader in that crazy dream.

That is where disruptive storytelling ramps up the challenge. It challenges every team member to embrace the dream and then accept the challenge to play a significant part. Disruptive storytelling requires crazy participation.

They don't just play a bit part but a significant role. They are not on the team just to follow along in the shadows but rather are thrust onto center stage.

The disruptive leader is wise to consider how to tell the story in the way, so followers willingly play a significant part. That requires conviction, energy, and authenticity.

You must believe the crazy story can become a reality. If you don't believe it, they won't engage.

Your story must have the energy to launch and finish the project. They need to hear that energy in your telling of the story.

Without authenticity, no one will believe your lofty vision or join you in pursuit. Share the lofty vision of what can be done and how everyone involved will benefit. Share as much of the strategy without bogging down in details. Telling the story is to share the hope and reveal the vision. It is the act of engaging your team to learn what everyone can do together and how they will make it happen.

Done right, disruptive storytelling helps them see how the future will be crazy fun.

Done wrong, disruptive storytelling convinces them you are crazy, and they need to stay away. It is too big and too risky. Why would they play a part in that craziness?

Hearing the crazy story and embracing the role will create a real challenge for many ordinary team members. That is why disruptive storytelling isn't just speaking but coming to a shared understanding, i.e., having everyone on the same page, playing out the same story.

That is not easy unless everyone believes they can do it.

### Interacting: Managing Conflict

Disruption creates internal and external conflict.

If you don't believe me, just mention a crazy big idea to your friends and wait for the push back. People are content following. They love to show how something is NOT going to work. Very few people want to challenge the status quo. Instead, most love to predict failure, especially when crazy success makes you look better than they do.

That means the disruptive leader building the cutting-edge team must be preventive and reactive to conflict.

Recently I was directing a play I wrote. I knew the situation. The approach of previous plays was wearing thin with our audience. to continue we would struggle to sell seats and get rave reviews. As someone who tracks the trends and forecasts the opportunities and the threats, I knew we either had to raise our standards and performance or quit. We had to go big or go home. We could not continue with the status quo.

I was exhilarated at the thought of what we could do. So, I shared my crazy vision. Initially, each actor voiced their enthusiasm and pledged their commitment. Silly me took their reaction at face value.

It wasn't long to see passive and active aggression. One actor rewrote her lines without consulting me as director or playwright. The problem was not only a disrespect for me as a leader which will kill any project but that she was changing the story line. To make matters worse, she wouldn't admit it and claimed ignorance.

I knew about this actor but like many organizational projects, there were reasons why I couldn't just get rid of her. As much as I knew it would damage the outcome, she was there to stay.

Naturally, if I had my way, I would have chosen an individual who had that collaborative attitude. I knew that belligerence blasts apart cutting-edge cultures. Adam Grant, author of *Give & Take*, wisely shows that one taker will kill a collaborative project. I knew that when I started but thought that if we did a few things different, she would come around and everything would work out great. I was wrong.

So, like the good, disruptive leader that I wanted to be, I sought to offset any future conflict by getting everyone to buy-in. I knew that creating a cutting-edge culture requires that we prepare for conflict.

However, I wasn't prepared for the belligerence that disruptive innovation provokes.

*Disruptive Tip: When choosing your team, look for attitude as much as talent.*

Belligerence is "a warlike or aggressively hostile nature, condition, or attitude." (Dictionary.com). It not only says, "I don't believe in your vision" or "I think it is better doing it my way" but that "you are bat crap crazy and I'm going to prove it."

Obviously, THAT is NOT collaboration.

If you sense belligerence in your disruptive team, that team member must go. Remember what Adam Grant said, one taker will ruin the project.

Much of the belligerence you will face as a disruptive leader will be passive-aggressive. They say they believe it, but their actions expose their hearts.

In my case, at almost every rehearsal or discussion in the play, she would counter my vision with her own. She was not only disengaged but actively disengaged.

You have the same disengaged employees; they just look different and go by a different name. The attitude is the same.

Why? Why do they push back? In my first book, I detailed 8 reasons why people embrace ordinary instead of the ultimate. Some cannot see the vision while others lack confidence, compelling motivation, or conviction. Still, others don't see how they can participate due to time or energy. Some can't move forward without seeing the process. Of course, the worst is when a team member doesn't believe the innovation you are promoting is good, healthy, or valuable.

Each of these reasons or excuses foster resistance. Sometimes you can tell the story in a way that provides more details in a way that engages them. But for many of these, the disruptive vision threatens their sense of safety and causes them to create conflict. Understand their fears and tell the story to alleviate their fears.

That is what I should have done from the beginning. The controlling person is fearful. It will be wearing but when you can alleviate their fears, they often join the ranks.

At the same time, some are belligerent because of ego. They must be in control and things must be done their way. In those cases, you must get rid of them because it will cease to be your vision. They will chip away until the vision is no longer crazy or good. It will be just another safe project. For any disruptive leader, that is the death of the project. You can counter almost any obstacle but a belligerent ego.

For the rest, we need to listen to their fears and aspirations.

In the end, I can blame this cast member, but the opportunity comes when I pivot from my ridged mindset to leverage their concerns and engage in a way where they find satisfaction. It is worth a try. It doesn't always work but will yield more success than not trying.

When your best efforts don't work, it is time to terminate the relationship. Unfortunately, too many felt trapped like I did. Pivot your perspective to see what that conflict is causing and manage it to seize your best opportunities.

**Listening:**

Listening is an exhilarating process. I love the process because it demands that we disconnect so we are open to the best opportunities. I also like listening because it is saturated with compassion. Those that follow me know that compassion is the absolute best business practice. This is especially true in building a cutting-edge culture.

In the very beginning as disruptive leaders, we listen to the creative muses that provide the innovative ideas. We open ourselves up to what can be instead of what is.

We also quiet our minds as we follow the trends and then look ahead to see where the opportunities will emerge. We lose our preconceived notions and are listening to the world and how it is operating.

Then we listen to our team. Who are they, why are they here and how would they like to be involved? In many ways, at this point, it is not about you as the disruptive leader but about them.

That is what makes for a cutting-edge team. That is where I made my mistake. I had a lofty vision and worked to share it with my team. Ultimately it worked but not to the level I desired. Had I done one of two things, it would have reached that level.

First, I could have brought everyone together and inductively worked to develop a disruptive vision. It would have then been their dream as much as mine. That would have ensured that they were committed.

Second, I needed to listen to them early on, understand their fears, and work individually with them to alleviate their fears. I needed them to know we were having a shared experience, not that I was forcing my experience on them. That is crucial.

Negotiating that shared meaning is a constant challenge at every point in the disruptive innovation. We do that best by setting aside our thoughts and convictions and listening authentically to them, even when we suspect we know the answer.

Listening starts by shutting up, calming our minds, and setting aside our ego.

But make no mistake. We never sacrifice the disruptive vision. We must maintain our ultimate standards. That means we often need to listen for new methods or different approaches.

Disruption brings conflict. The very notion of doing something that no one has ever done before will bring out the critics, even in what you thought were loyal team members. There are several reasons for that conflict that we will discuss in the next few posts on disruptive attitudes, beliefs and values.

In the end, when we quiet our minds and listen to ourselves, our team, and the possibilities in trends, we can build cutting-edge teams that do amazing things.

While this last project didn't reach the heights that I desired, I stopped and listened, understanding what happened and what role I played. I maintain my lofty vision, even raising it beyond just doing plays to making movies. To do what I want to do, I know what I need to do. I need to tell a compelling story, accept there will be conflict and listen carefully to manage that conflict. I need to speak, interact, and listen. In the process, I cannot forfeit my vision.

Effective communication requires understanding how language impacts our audience in the next normal.

## Choose Your Language Carefully

Language is critical for creating a shared meaning. If we use words that others don't recognize, we haven't communicated. If we use words to mean something different than the other person does, we haven't communicated.

Businesses have 3 choices in Tough Times: Reset, Pivot, or Leap.

**A Critical Decision**

Any disruption stops us in our tracks. At that point, we have three choices. You can reset, go back to the way you were working, pivot by adding a new product or service, or leap forward to a completely new opportunity.

**Reset**

To reset is to return to a previous point and work from there. This is when a computer program or electronic device quits working and needs to be reset to the previous settings to work effectively.

As individuals who have just lost a loved one, a job, or physical abilities, we want life to return to what it was before the loss.

As businesses who have just suffered a setback, we want life to return to when business was great.

Even if it is impossible to return to the previous normal there are ways we can reset.

Return to what you know best.
Return to the habits that brought you job.
Return to your values.
Return to what your customers need and want.
Return to your best practices of operation that still work.

*PIVOTAL LEADERS*

You can reset to a previous, simpler way of living or doing business. Maybe it is reviving an old friendship, reading a favorite book, or looking through old photographs. In business maybe it is reviving a former marketing perspective or product. Sometimes, resetting to an earlier way of working works better is just what you need to get moving.

For example, during the shutdown, some people went back to what their parents or grandparents did, cooking for themselves. That is a different type of resetting. So many learned how to make bread that there was a yeast shortage. Others improved their cooking. Still others learned how to paint by watching vintage Bob Ross videos.

By working from home, many reset to a different age and enjoyed better work-life balance. They spent more time as a family and became reacquainted.

Some wise business leaders reset their approach to marketing by reaching out to former customers. They didn't make sales a priority, instead option simply to connect and see how they could help. Resetting to come alongside others in their pain is the best way to engage your employees, vendors, and customers.

CAUTION: Don't think you can simply go back to the way things were. These crises that I like to call "economic earthquakes" leave some structures of our lives in rubble, never able to be revived. With the exposure to widespread virtual work, we will find some traditional ways of working obsolete. Not changing is not an option. Recognize that failing to change and clinging to our old, comfortable yet antiquated mindsets and practices will spell doom for us.

In what ways can you reset to reinforce your values, beliefs, and relationships?

In what ways can you reset to increase your performance, productivity, and profits?

**Pivot**

To pivot is to keep one foot in place while we swivel to change perspective and position. Think of the basketball player dribbling the ball up court and being cornered by an opponent. He stops dribbling to avoid the turnover. The player has one choice at this point – pass the ball to a teammate or call timeout.

Any trauma or setback stops us in our tracks. We pivot because we cannot do a complete reset. Returning to exactly the way things once worked is no longer a viable option. Circumstances demand that we change. The safest way to change is to pivot forward.

Sometimes we pivot because we are too hesitant to let go and leap. We appreciate the current situation but recognize the potential ahead. Before we even think about leaping, we pivot to see what else is available. Like the basketball player guarded by an opponent, we pivot quickly seeking our next opportunity. We pivot to change our focus and get a clear vision of the potential opportunities.

Pivoting creates three challenges. First, if we pivot too quickly, we may lose our balance and forfeit our success. Second, we must look and work quickly to find the next viable opportunity. Meanwhile, we must also keep that one foot planted on our current business. Third, the current situation doesn't allow us to stand still. We don't have any choice but to pivot. We must make our new choices quickly.

For example, following the pandemic shutdown, many traditional businesses are forced to consider employees working remotely. They didn't have any choice. They were shutdown. To do nothing meant they would go out of business. Many made that choice.

However, others pivoted quickly. Traditional sit-down restaurants quickly expanded their offerings to provide takeout and curbside pickup. Tampa's Forbici Modern Italian restaurant realized they had access to a toilet paper supplier with plenty of inventory. Jeff Gigante quickly pivoted to begin offering a roll of toilet paper with every order. Now that's a pivot.

Relators faced a dire situation when they couldn't show houses. That meant owners couldn't sell. The savvy ones quickly adopted technology that allowed potential buyers to tour the home via video. Meanwhile, some threw up their hands, sat on the couch, and binge watched their new favorite show. They chose not to reset or to pivot but instead quit.

On a personal note, losing a loved one causes many to stop. They feel paralyzed but the hole left in their lives. At this point, the only thing we can consider is survival. We can't think about pivoting in those early days. But at some point, we must take the safe step into the future. It is more difficult for some than others. We don't want to let go of the past. That's why the pivot is so important. We keep one foot anchored in that past while pivoting the other into the future.

To make a pivot, from a personal or business perspective, ask these questions. (The last two are specifically for business.)

- What are our choices?
- Which one is the most beneficial?
- If so, how will it help?
- What resources will be needed?
- What do I have that others need?
- Who can help?
- What policies are needed?
- Can we ensure continued performance, production, and profits?

Notice I didn't include, "When is the best time?" Normally SMART goals include that. But in Tough Times, you need to act NOW. Pivoting is essential in those moments.

A word of caution: In business, we always want to be strategic and not reactionary. We do need to act quickly in Tough Times but pivoting to the Next Normal cannot be a frantic, kneejerk decision. Instead, bring your team together, listen carefully, and then pivot quickly. This is no time for "paralysis by analysis" nor is it time for impulsive actions. Balance the timing. At the same time, be prepared to fail quickly. Make your best decision, implement it quickly, and use the shortest amount of time to determine its value. Don't stick with something if it isn't working.

Ella Bing, a Tampa haberdashery quickly realized that they only sold what people wanted, not what they needed. No one was shopping at their store. Knowing they needed to pivot, they quickly began making and selling fabric facemasks. Meanwhile, the owner Brent Kraus began researching and then offering recession proof products.

In the same way, distilleries quickly pivoted to provide hand sanitizers and automobile manufacturers began making ventilators.

**Leap**

A leap is the biggest and boldest move. To leap is to leave the spot where you were standing and propel yourself to a new place. That takes considerable effort and planning. We leap in two different settings, when there is no other choice or because we want to get to a place that is much better.

Many are afraid to lead, especially after suffering a trauma. worried about trying and failing. Fear of the fall prevents them from ever taking the leap. For those looking for stability, leaping is inadvisable.

But what about personal trauma. Josh Opperman returned to his New York City apartment to find his fiancé had only left and the engagement ring. The heartbreak was bad enough but then he found the jeweler would only give him 35% of the $30,000 ring. He pivoted by starting a website, "I Do . . . Now I Don't" where he sells rings from broken relationships. From this emotional trauma, he leaped to establish a lucrative business. Now that's not just a reset or a pivot. It's a leap.

Then there is Chad Hymas. He was young and healthy, working on his Utah farm, lifting a 2000 bale with his tractor and loader. Something went wrong and the bale fell, shattering his neck and leaving him paralyzed. Without the use of his legs, he leaped into becoming a hall of fame speaker, one of the top motivational speakers in the world, and bestselling author, while traveling 300,000 miles a year. What a leap.

Sometimes we have no other choice than to leap. If our house is burning and we are on the second floor with no other viable choices, we must leap.

At other times, we leap because we want to. As a child, it was fun to run and leap, flying through the air to get to where we wanted quicker. As adults, we don't run and leap as much as we once did.

**Your Challenge**

Learn to think bigger.

Maybe returning during the Tough Times is the perfect opportunity to take a little leap into the Next Normal.

Maybe this is the time to reset our sense of adventure and decide what we ultimately want.

Maybe this is the time when we as business leaders make the leap and embrace innovative thinking.

At the same time, maybe this is the time to embrace a more compassionate style of leadership.

Maybe this is the time where you realize how antiquated your company has become. If so, this is the time to make the bold leap forward.

# 8: SHARE YOUR INNOVATIVE VISION

We pivot to clarify our vision for the future. To leap, we had better know where were hoped to land. However, traumatic times often blind us to what is possible.

In calmer times, having an innovative vision is exciting. As a leader, we have a vision and then share that vision with our team. The challenge is to share that vision in a way that convinces them to jump on board.

But what about during the tough times? How do we do that when others are apprehensive? How do we share a vision when they are afraid of the future?

**What Do You See?**

Great innovative leaders seem to have a crystal ball and see into the future. What do they see what others don't? How do they see it?

Many see the world without the persistent problem. They may envision a world of absence of pain, struggle or evil. Even though they cannot see exactly how, when, or where they have a vision of freedom from that problem.

Some see the world from a different perspective. They willingly shift to consider the current world from a seldom viewed angle. Where others see the status quo, they see a new opportunity.

Still others track trends and look ahead to see where that trend will take them. They see the world incrementally or exponentially better. At some point in the future, they see an opportunity to do what they ultimately desire.

Then there are those that look to the past and see opportunities for the present and the future. They re-imagine what others have discarded.

Still others see exciting opportunities to do what they have always wanted to do. These "bucket list" desires are tucked away in the not-too-distant part of their brains, waiting for the right opportunity.

During it all, leaders see opportunities to solve problems. They make the world better by making it more enjoyable, less stressful, or simply easier. That is critical to sharing the vision with their team.

In my 3rd book, *Now What? Secrets to Sensing New Opportunities When You Need Them Most*, I detail how Tough Times helps us to expand our vision.

**Embracing Your Dream**

In my first book, *Chevettes to Corvettes*, *(Pivotal Small Business)* I detail how a dream is the wispy, emotional beginning of an engaging idea for what could be. It is the bud that blossoms into a vision with the proper attention.

Most leaders don't use the word "dream" as it has connotations of wasted time thinking about unicorn and pink elephant fantasies. Instead, they choose to focus on the "reality" of business.

I disagree. Dreams drive innovation. Dreams are those emotional aspects of our lives that propel us further than we would proceed on logic alone. Left alone, they are mere daydreaming. However, when they are engaged with effort and logic, they develop into valuable innovations.

Look into any great innovator and you will find what drives them. It might be a competitive desire to be the first or a curiosity that is fanned into a flame. The dream is that airy, fragile imagination that intrigues and then drives us to do what we have never done. That requires that we not just think or talk about the dream but to act. That requires building a team and sharing the vision.

Dreams are also extremely valuable and world changing when we pass through difficult times. As I explain in *Making More Money in Tough*

## PIVOTAL LEADERS

*Times_(Pivotal Paradigm Shift)* and *The ROI of Compassion (Pivotal Compassion)*. We can dream when we when we can do nothing else. Paralyzed by trauma, we dream of what used to be and how we wished it could be. Those dreams keep us sane and somewhat balanced in those terrifying times. But they also do something much more powerful. They drive us to act. Many leaders have changed the world because they suffered and had a dream. Martin Luther King, Jr. uttered those famous words, "I have a dream" on the steps of the Lincoln Memorial out of the pain of slavery. It was that dream that drove him and many others to do what others never thought possible.

What is your dream?

### Developing the Vision

Your dream becomes an innovative vision when you apply the logic, give it detail, and work to make it reality. The dream drives but the vision forges the future. The vision is the blueprint for the change.

Anyone who has built their dream house dreams of an experience. That dream becomes reality when they give the dream detail for each room. The dream begins to take shape when the architect draws up the plans, determining the size of each room and drawing up the plans. The designer then adds the pizzazz with the colors, furnishings, and landscaping.

Notice the two steps. First, the architect makes the dream functional. The architect ensures the dream is safe and functional. They work out the minute details. Second, the designers work to find exactly the right colors for each room, plants for each bed, stonework, and all the other details inside and outside the house.

In the end, the dream becomes the vision when the plan is detailed.

How detailed is your vision?

### Sharing the Vision

Martin Luther King, Jr. shared his dream. He didn't hide it, or simply enjoy it. One of the first questions I ask my executive coaching clients is, "What is your dream?" They are often puzzled, expecting to think more logically. They are also a bit hesitant to share what they ultimately desire. That all changes when we work to develop that dream into their vision. Developing that vision gives them the confidence to share that vision with their team.

Sharing is a critical component. for creating a cutting-edge culture. We build teams because we cannot do great things by ourselves. We are wise to remember that the best innovative teams are engaged, committed and in sync with a vision that they embrace. In other words, they share our vision. Sharing is "taking part in" an experience.

This is critical.

Sharing is not telling them what to embrace. Instead, sharing is voluntarily joining someone else, giving of ourselves, working together. Sharing is not demanding obedience. MLK's speech was so powerful because he shared a dream that millions of Americans already embraced. In the same way, innovative leaders share their vision in a way that taps into the dreams of their team. They know what they are building and are willing to freely share it with their team.

Sharing implies openness, transparency and, to some degree, vulnerability. Innovation is not an exact science and there will be mistakes. Being vulnerable means setting aside judgment and punishment. To share a vision is to welcome an opportunity to attempt something that has not been done before, at least within your organization.

Share your vision with your team to build the collaboration and camaraderie necessary to create.

How willing are you to share? How willing is your team to share?

**Engaging Your Team**

Engagement is being totally involved, committed and willing. Innovative leaders create cutting-edge cultures by sharing their dreams and vision but also by encouraging their team to share. That requires a safe environment. No one shares if they are criticized or punished.

We all know that collaboration requires sharing of ideas. There is a communal atmosphere saturated with individual accolades. We work together for a common goal and even share resources but give credit where credit is due. There isn't a competitive, cutthroat "me first" mentality but rather a synergistic, pooling of talents and energy. That vulnerability is a closely held value.

In my research, I have found that cutting-edge cultures have employees who are willing to share their dreams and those dreams are celebrated. They have all bought into and share the corporate vision but that comes because the vision fits their dreams. We each have dreams for how we want our lives to be. When a team member sees how that corporate vision fits their dream, they are engaged.

Unfortunately, too many organizations fail to see the value of those individual dreams. They violate those individual visions of success by squeezing all the creativity and vulnerability out and creating a sterile workplace. No wonder they don't innovate.

Innovative organizations have a vision of doing what has never been done before. They see a new world and are compelled to make that vision a reality.

- What is your dream?
- How will it change the world?
- When will you share it with your team?

**A Disruptive Vision**

Imagine inspiring the homeless to take up running. The very thought is disconnected. We are used to seeing the homeless population sitting, laying or slowly moving. Meanwhile, we see those who purposely run several miles a day. That seems to be an opposite pair of imagines. It also seems to be an impossible task to get the homeless to run and re-enter society.

But that's what Anne Mahlum did. While trying to work through her own personal issues following the divorce of her parents, she enjoyed daily runs through downtown Philadelphia. One day she happened to notice several members of a homeless camp along her usual route. One made a comment and she responded. Over the next few runs, she bantered with them and began to develop a relationship.

That's when she had the breakthrough idea. "I wonder if I could get the homeless to run."

In her 2013 TEDx Talk, she detailed why so many believed her title, "There is No Way This Will Work." Who would? I wouldn't have thought it would work. It still makes me smile because it was so far outside of my reality.

This story is a great example of a disruptive dream that became a vision. It is disruptive because it is radically changing the lives and the culture. If successful, Mahlum would help these men and women re-enter society. That's significant but it's also well beyond the realm of reality for most.

Visionary leaders dream these dreams and ask these types of questions.

Later you will read how she constructed a successful strategy. In the process she worked to leverage their fear and pain.

**Your Challenge**
>Have you been thinking too small?
>How have you ignored or overlooked great opportunities?
>Maybe it's the perfect time for you to reach higher.

# 9: LEVERAGE FEAR

Remembering good times provides a good escape during difficult times. Dreaming of what could have been or what we ultimately want is also a good escape and can help develop that vision for the future. However, focusing on what could have been or what we would like to be can cause considerable fear and pain.

Earlier I mentioned Aaron Burros who challenged himself to run 50 marathons in 50 states in 50 weeks following a near fatal armed robbery. In that moment when he was threatened and then as he was shot five times, he feared he would die. He survived but now suffers from PTSD. As he runs, he always encounters the pain from a bullet fragment left in his glute muscle. Maybe even worse, as the pain increases, the PTSD kicks in, reprising the fear from that fateful night five years before. To go forward, he uses every physical and emotional ounce of energy to leverage that pain into a blessing. He is the #runningservant who is running to bring healing to himself and others by raising funds for research and treatment at St. Jude's Hospital.

Very few of us can identify with Aaron's level of intense physical or emotional pain. However, we do understand the pain of Tough Times. What we need to learn is how to leverage that pain into leading in that Next Normal.

## PIVOTAL LEADERS

**The Process of Leverage**

Growing up on a farm, I learned to leverage at an early age. Any time we were faced with moving something that was too heavy or too difficult to grab, we went for our trust five-footlong, rounded pry bar. Next, we found a wooden or cement block, maybe even a big rock for a fulcrum. From there we put the bar as far under the object as possible, adjusted the fulcrum for the best positioning, and pushed down. Levers allow anyone to multiply their strength.

We need leverage when facing our fears because they are often much bigger than our faith. By leveraging our fear, we have two choices. First, we can use the leverage to move them out of the way. Second, we can use our fears to drive us to think bigger and reach higher. Leverage is one of the primary ways we do what we never thought possible.

The pivotal process uses collaboration to sense and seize the best opportunities in the future. However, many are frozen by fear of the unknown in that future. They look back and grieve what has been lost. They look at the present and dread potential consequences of something not predictable, comfortable, or safe.

That was much the same was as a little boy on a farm would look before he learned about leverage. "That's too big. What will I do now?" By learning leverage, that little boy can move rocks exceeding his body weight.

In the same way, leaders who leverage their team strengths will move mountains. Part of that leverage will come in facing fears. Fear is the potential for pain. Notice it is not the reality of current pain but rather worrying about future pain. Fear is debilitating doubt about being able to handle what might happen. Notice two key words. Read that sentence again. Fear is *debilitating doubt* about being able to handle what *might* happen. First fear is debilitating. It immobilizes and deactivates us. Second, we are disabled due to doubt, an inability to believe in our success. Third, this debilitating doubt is all fostered by what we believe might happen. Worry is praying for what we don't want. Instead of working for what we want to happen, we tremble thinking about the trauma that could possibly happen in the future.

Doesn't that seem silly?

We can conquer our fears when we surround ourselves with people, communication, and strategy that works to deliver the best success. In other words, sound strategy and hard work increases the odds of success. Diligent work leads to success which diminishes doubt.

**No Pain – No Gain**

To understand how to leverage pain, we examine someone who purposely puts himself in painful situations. You might wonder, "Why would anyone do that?"

They do it to seize incredible opportunities. Athletes purposely push themselves into and through pain to become winners. To strengthen their muscles and prepare for competition, they need to push themselves far beyond their comfort zones and leverage that pain into peak performance. Without the pain, there would be no gain.

That ability to perform through pain is seen in several courageous performances.

- Tiger Woods won the 2008 US Open while playing 91 holes on a broken leg and torn ACL.
- Gymnast Keri Strug helped the 1996 US Olympic team win gold with a stellar performance on the vault despite having sprained her ankle just before the competition. Her ankle hurst so badly her coach had to carry her off the floor.
- Michael Jordon scored 38 points in game 5 of the 1997 NBA finals despite having the flu.
- Los Angeles Ram's player Jack Youngblood broke his leg during the second quarter of a 1979 NFL playoff game. Not only did he stay in the game, but he played two more playoff games. He went on to play in the Pro Bowl
- The NFL 49er's defensive back Ronnie Lott broke his left pinky finger tackling a Dallas Cowboy running back in the last game of the season. Not wanting to forfeit his chance to help his team in a Wildcard playoff game, the physician gave him a choice. Do surgery and put a pin in it but miss the playoffs. Option two was to amputate the finger at the knuckle. Lott chose the latter and played.

Those athletes leveraged pain to reach their Next Normal level of success. They played through the pain because they trained by leveraging their pain. That is what led them to winning.

## PIVOTAL LEADERS

**Surf Photography**

There is another individual who chooses to play in an environment filled with bone chilling pain. Chris Burkard calls himself a surf photographer. As he started his career, he had a dream job traveling to exotic, tropical beaches. What a life.

Then he purposely pivoted, taking his professional photography to another level. He launched a crusade against the mundane by purposely pushing himself to explore the best waves in the world. That required that he leave the topics and travel to the most extreme places on the planet. It also led to him expanding his work and influence. No longer just a photographer, he pivoted to become an accomplished explorer, photographer, creative director, speaker, author, and worldwide influencer. His TED Talk title says it all, "Joy of Surfing in Ice Cold Water."

Doesn't that sound crazy? To most of us, there would be no joy purposely seeking cold weather much less surfing in ice cold water. But for Burkard, he not only tolerated it but grew to love it. Purposely diving into frigid water required him to find value in pain.

That's the question we need to ask ourselves, "what is the value of the pain we are suffering?"

Too often we fail to try to create the radical change and attempt the disruptive innovation because we fear some sort of pain. Too often we see pain for only the negative, especially when we are in the middle of an exceedingly difficult period.

**5 Lessons**

From these lessons and others, we can see there are five lessons to learn about leveraging pain.

1. Our comfortable world becomes mundane if there is no challenge or pain.

Burkard became bored doing what everyone else was clamoring to do. That monotony became painful and that pushed him to go to the extreme.

Did you become board during the shutdown?

At what point did you get tired of the pain from a personal trauma?

At what point did you want to live again?

2. Pain pushes us out of our comfort zone and demands radical change.

Burkard felt like he was suffocating working in the world of comfort and ease. It was not until he sought out the extreme that he found his joy.

The Tough Times push us out of our comfort zones. What changes can we make to embrace the Next Normal?

How can you help others leave their comfort zone? Learning to live again can be extremely painful. Help them leverage their pain to lead their Next Normal.

How can you capitalize on the adjustments you made during Tough Times?

3. Disruptive Leaders seek out the Extreme and expect the pain.

Each of the individuals mentioned in this chapter spent years pushing themselves through pain. They sought out the most difficult challenges in preparation for their best opportunities. Instead of avoiding pain, they sought it out, expected it, welcomed it, and finally leveraged it.

How do you already welcome pain for what you want the most?

How did the Tough Times help you to leverage the pain?

4. Pain pushes us to the Next Normal.

Burkard stated in his TED Talk that he found shivering to be a form of meditation. That sounds crazy, doesn't it? But when he looks back at being so cold that he could feel the blood leaving his lips and extremities, he found a focus that he never had before. He leveraged the pain of shivering into a state where his senses were heightened. That pushed him to a New Normal.

The purpose of pain isn't to punish but to push us to our Next Normal stage of living and working. Without that pain, we would maintain our mediocre success.

When I began running in my late 50s, many questioned my motives. One friend asked, "What is your goal? Bad knees or a bad heart." He couldn't understand why anyone would purposely get off the couch and push themselves into pain. He didn't understand the purpose of pain.

Why would Aaron Burros purposely push himself into a setting where his PTSD might be triggered? Because there is a greater goal. He is raising funds to fight diseases that kill kids. It's worth his pain to help others.

How can you leverage your pain to help others?

What is the purpose of your pain?

5. Pain requires sacrifice.

Burkard says that one of his favorite parts of going to the extreme was the challenge of getting there. Reaching those remote beaches in Norway, Russia and Chile pushed him to his limits of creativity and perseverance.

Jerry Rice was known for his work ethic. He was often the first player to practice and stayed long after the rest were finished. Is there any wonder he helped his team win multiple Super Bowls and was named to the NFL Hall of Fame?

When Keri Strug stepped on the mat for her last opportunity on the vault, she was in pain. To help her team and to accomplish her individual goals, she had to sacrifice her comfort.

What part of your current world are you willing to sacrifice to create your ultimate success?

Difficult times demand sacrifice to survive. Those that are willing to leverage their pain often do what others never thought possible.

Are you one of those rare individuals?

Are you willing to leverage your pain to lead your Next Normal? If so, we need to link our word with action.

**Your Challenge**

What are you afraid of?

What breakthrough opportunity do you see in working though this fear?

# 10: LEVERAGE PAIN

Navigating into the Next Normal, especially as a business leader, requires engaging others in pain. In this chapter, we will discuss the five messages that disengage even the most loyal team members if your actions do not match your words.

Communication, creating shared meaning with words, symbols, gestures, and the like, is leveraging our words to help alleviate their pain. Our goal is to help others take the lead in the Next Normal.

In business, communication becomes a critical problem because most employees are disengaged to some degree. According to the 2017 Gallup State of the American Workplace, only a third of workers are fully engaged. That means that they are likely hearing a different message than you intend.

Personally, we have become a politically polarized country that believes our opinions trump proven facts. Our social media and individual cell phones foster a self-centered perspective compared to the shared, antiquated, home telephone. We expect more individual attention, especially from our leaders. In other words, we as a culture have become very self-centered. Right or wrong, that is the world we live in as Pivotal Leaders.

## Team Member Pain

As I write this, the political tensions and COVID pandemic have created a massive divide that won't be fused quickly or easily. As leaders, that is our challenge. We must work to alleviate pain to create cutting-edge teams. We can't work together if we are denying the other's pain. Appreciate the pain of both sides because each perspective offers part of the solution.

On one side, we have those that don't fear the virus. Their pain is the fear of losing personal and financial freedom. They fear losing their jobs to an unnecessary shutdown. They fear the pain of not being able to gather with friends and family inside and outside of work. They fear their lifestyle is being threatened by an overreaching government. Some fear the pain of a shift away from democracy to socialism or even communism.

Think beyond the pandemic. These are the individuals that are willing to take the risks. You need them and their attitude. They are the ones that are more likely to welcome the opportunities in the Next Normal.

As a leader, feel their pain. Understand what they are afraid of losing.

During the pandemic, fear permeated from each side. On one, we had those very fearful of the virus. They feared becoming one of the half million that would die in the first year in the United States. They feared their loved ones would be one of those statistics. So they gladly quarantined and wore masks. They would do whatever it took help flatten the curve. Meanwhile, they feared the consequences of those refusing to comply. Even after vaccinations, they live cautiously with the fear of something happening.

Meanwhile, the other side feared economic failure and suppression of their rights. They were so fearful that they denied scientific expert testimony. They discredited anyone who didn't believe as they did. Fear does that. The fear stuck in the limbic system overrides the logical conclusions in the frontal neocortex of the brain.

Notice the two extremes. I'm not here to say which is correct. Time will tell us that. My point is that there are always those who deny the need for change and those who have an urgency for change. There will be those who take risks and those that won't. Some will be willing to pivot but need some assurance. Others welcome the challenge and

# PIVOTAL LEADERS

adopt the hard charging, "damn the torpedoes, full speed ahead" approach.

The wide Pivotal Leader provides a balance, recognizing that both sides have their strengths and flaws.

As Pivotal Leaders, our challenge to work with every team member where they are. That is the cornerstone of success as a leader in the Next Normal. Compassionate leadership will reveal far more opportunities than competitive, selfish leadership.

**Compassionate Leadership**

As we have discussed earlier, compassion is coming alongside another to help alleviate their pain. Compassionate leaders notice the pain of the team, then feel their pain from the team member's perspective. Those two elements create empathy. While empathy is nice, it does not motivate workers. Compassion adds strategic thinking and action alleviate those pains. Remember, the four steps are notice, feel, think, and act.

I repeat this because the process is often violated and leaders wonder why employees are not engaging. If your team is disengaged, if you can't seem to get them onboard, you need to examine what pain you haven't addressed.

Is Your Team ENGAGED?
If not, could your leaderhip style be the Weak Link?

*Loren Murfield, Ph.D.*
*www.MurfieldCoaching.com*

## Balancing Compassion

That's not to say that leaders are solely responsible for alleviating every pain. It's your job to HELP alleviate their pain. They must have a stake in the game. They must be willing to solve their pain. In other words, compassion takes collaboration.

A word of caution. The challenge of being a compassionate leader is understanding which pain(s) to address. Some people magnifiy even the smallest of pains and expect others to solve them. The challenge is to know what pain you can help alleviate and which ones are their responsibility. You also need to know which pain requires professional help. Finding that balance of compassion is extremely difficult.

Remember, your goal as a leader in business or in the community, is to help your team pivot and leap into the Next Normal. Finding that balance of which pains to address and which to leave for their own maybe the most difficult part of leadership.

## Compassionate Communication

You read it earlier, but it needs to be repeated. We often communicate to reduce uncertainty, and there is a lot of uncertainty right now.

Communication is defined as "negotiating shared meaning between two very different people." In our aim to help alleviate their pain, we need to understand how different we are and how much we need to listen to understand their pain. We also need to be aware of how our words may misunderstood if we have not built trust in the past.

Disengaged employees are created by leaders who haven't taken the time to help alleviate their pain. Our actions speak much louder than our words. The actions you take will tell every member of your team whether you value them or if they are simply cogs in the organizational machine.

However, your words do matter. Everyone interprets a message through their own world and experience. If they are disengaged, they will likely take a skeptical approach to whatever you say.

In studying communication during traumatic events, especially returning to work following the COVID pandemic, I've found five phrases that are best avoided, especially when trying to alleviate their pain. You may initially think, "Why is that phrase a problem?" You may also wonder if I'm a member of the cancel culture and overly concerned about offending.

That's not my point.

In each of the five phrases, you will find a dishonesty. Pivotal Leadership is authentic and transparent to help alleviate pain and navigate into the Next Normal. Look farther and you will see that these five phrases are often used to "get everyone onboard" a new project. Unfortunately, they are often used to "twist the arms" and get your way.

As a word of perspective, my focus in my communication studies master's and Ph.D. studies focused on the emotional power of language to create and destroy. Words matter greatly.

**First, "It's Your Choice."**

As organizations began to open following the pandemic shutdown, many used this message. Leaders intended for their employees to hear, "We care about you and don't want you harmed. It's your choice whether to return to work now or later." You want your team to know you care and don't want to push them into a decision.

However, disengaged employees hear, "Sure it is. You may say the choice is up to us, but will there be repercussions for choosing to stay home or deviate from returning when you say? I'm not sure I can trust you."

If your organizational culture expects team members to sacrifice for the good of the organization, they don't really have a choice. They know you don't mean what you say. To do anything other than what you want means choosing to look for another job.

The only way, "it's your choice" is valuable is if you have already established that the team member has a legitimate choice and there will be no repercussions for doing what they think is best.

Say instead: "Given your situation, what do you think is best to do?"

**Second, "You are a valuable part of our team."**

The message you want them to hear is, "The most productive teams collaborate and sacrifice to achieve incredible results. I'm assuming you want to be on a winning team."

The message disengaged employees hear is, "You don't really care about me, you just care about results. So, what do you want me to do now? What sacrifice do you want today?"

Developing an engaged team requires trust. Once the team trusts each other, they will gladly sacrifice. But requiring sacrifice without trust breeds contempt. What do your team members hear when they hear this?

Instead, say, "We value the work you do and what you bring to the team. However, we want you to be comfortable returning to the workplace. What concerns do you have?"

**Third, "We have your best interest in mind."**

The message you want them to hear is, "We care about you. You can come to us with any of your concerns."

The message disengaged employees hear is, "Yeah right. You have never had my best interest in mind. You just care about how much work you can get out of me."

If your organizational culture has never had the best interest of your employees in mind, it is best to avoid this phrase. Earn the right to say it. Feel their pain from their perspective.

Instead, say, "What concerns do you have about _____."

**Fourth, "You don't need to worry."**

This message is common far beyond the workplace. Any new risk involves risk and failing to appreciate that risk is foolishness. Telling someone who has concerned not to worry might be well intended but often ineffective.

It just doesn't work. Telling someone not to worry is like telling them not to think about purple elephants. That's all they think about. Besides, it doesn't alleviate the pain of their fears. If they could just stop worrying, they would have already done it. So, telling them not to worry is not only failing to be compassionate, but also telling them you are smarter than them. While some leaders feel that way, it isn't a wise leadership perspective.

The message you want them to hear is, "We have it under control. You don't need to worry about anything."

The message disengaged employees hear is, "That's why I worry. You have proven you don't have it under control and when it goes bad, as it usually does, guess who must pick up the pieces? Me. Yeah, I'm worried, and I should be. Look at the history."

Telling another not to worry is dismissing their pain. Very few trust another just because they say, "You can trust me." As an old friend once told me, "Whenever someone tells me to trust them, I hang on to my wallet." He was wise. Telling someone "Trust me" ignores the important details. If you have to say it, they probably cannot trust you. Trust is earned.

Instead, say, "What are you most concerned about?"

**Fifth, "We think it's best."**

This message might be the most belittling and dismissing. The message you want them to hear is, "Our management team has researched this extensively and have determined the best action."

For the faithful, that is good news. From past experience, they have come to know and trust you to do your homework.

However, the disengaged employees hears, "Ok, this is yet another time where you make the decisions, and we don't have a say. We should just obey you and assume everything will turn out fine. But you won't pay the price if I get sick or need to find daycare for my kids who are home from school. You haven't even considered my concerns, yet you claim to know what's best for me. What do you think I am, an idiot?"

Does that sound harsh? If so, that's because you are asking them to accept the conclusion to an important decision without providing any of the criteria or the process. Remember, Pivotal Leadership is transparent and authentic. Failing to share information creates questions. Refusing to share information automatically creates a distrust. Claiming to know what is best for everyone without hearing their perspective or considering their current or potential pain is anything but compassionate.

Instead, say, "Here is what we have been researching. We would like to hear your perspective."

## PIVOTAL LEADERS

I know some leaders will bristle at this and even claim I don't appreciate their position or how leadership works. I understand that leaders have been accustomed to being more of a dictator than a facilitator. I also understand that many followers want someone else to make those decisions. There are also many followers that want to take the passive approach and do as little as possible.

However, leaders who have shown compassion and celebrate the value of each team member enjoy a far higher team engagement. Team members appreciate working for an organization that values them, their perspective, and creative ideas. At the same time, who wants to give more if they are overlooked, neglected, or even ridiculed.

### An Example

During the pandemic, I was in a polite conversation with a small business professional. He claims to have made considerable money in his previous career. He was one of those "Sheldon Coopers" from the popular TV show, "Big Bang Theory." He openly said he was extremely smart and knew more about certain topics than most.

What's your reaction to someone like that?

As the conversation progressed, he explained his view on mask wearing. "I believe that I have superior genes and won't catch the disease."

Taken back by his arrogance, I pressed to see if he was as unsympathetic as it sounded.

"But masks are to protect others. Isn't their health a concern?"

"No. If they catch the virus and die, that just shows they have inferior genes. That's their problem, not mine."

From previous conversations, I knew his style of leadership was the draconian, "My way or the highway." He bragged that he was hired to help a company turnaround and promptly fired more than half of the employees. Granted, Tough Times often requires drastic action, but he didn't express an ounce of sympathy for their situation.

Unfortunately, he's not the only one that operated from this calloused mindset. My wife ran across several examples when researching our book, The *ROI of Compassion (Pivotal Compassion)*.

One company held a fire drill and asked everyone to leave the building. Then they announced that those employees whose access cards still worked could return to work. The rest were terminated.

**Your Challenge**

Communication is not an exact science. Think bigger to leverage your leadership power by being transparent and authentic. Build their trust by matching your words and actions. Then you can strategize your pivot or leap into the Next Normal.

# 11: BE AGGRESSIVE IN YOUR STRATEGY

A few chapters back you read about Anne Mahlum and her dream and vision to get the homeless to run.

When you watch the video of her TEDx Talk from Kansas City, you see that she first leveraged their pain. By first identifying with them, she could feel their pain from their perspective. That was critical for developing her strategy.

### Back on Your Feet

I love this story and find it to be a critical step in Pivotal Leadership. Mahlum finished her run while contemplating her strategy. She started by asking if she could get the homeless to run. That immediately triggered the question, "Has any one ever done that?"

Leading into the Next Normal often brings the response she heard, "No. No one has ever done it." Fortunately, she asked the homeless advocates and also heard, "If you want to, go for it." That is critical. First, asking the right people, not just friends and family that have other agendas. Second, receiving their encouragement to try is vital to going forward. Imagine if she had heard the stereotypical caution when suggesting a major leap, "Good luck with that. It will never work."

However, with Mahlum's connection to their pain, she had the motivation to do what others never imagined. It also gave her a strategy that others didn't consider.

First, she asked her running community for old shoes. After collecting them, she realized that plan wouldn't work. Mahlum imagined being on the receiving end. While the nearly worn-out shoes were better than nothing, would it inspire them to run? It was then that she pivoted from her original idea with a better idea, get sponsors to donate new shoes. Imagine the joy of a homeless man or woman receiving a new pair of running shoes.

Her next step involved creating a process to help them pivot their own lives. She didn't want them to run once and quit. Instead, Mahlum wanted them to find the same joy, inspiration, and healing from daily running that she did. It was her sanctuary for her healing, and she imagined it could be for some of them as well. She designed what turned out to be a pivotal program focused on recognition and personal accountability. First, she was a private citizen, not a government program, inviting them to run with her. She already had rapport with a few of the members so there was an element of trust. Second, she offered new, free shoes, to make running possible. Third, there were held accountable by posting their names and involvement for all to see. Fourth, she celebrated their success.

You won't be surprised to learn that it did worked. The homeless joined her and over time, many found the inspiration and courage to leave the streets and re-enter society. It worked so well that she started her not-for-profit organization, Back on My Feet, that now serves 14 cities.

In the end, Mahlum wasn't so crazy in asking that question, "Can I get the homeless to run?"

**Next Normal Strategy**

Many great business opportunities are ignored because someone doesn't see a solution or think it will work. The Next Normal contains challenges never seen before and solutions that haven't worked before. That's why we need to disrupt our thinking and innovate. New problems often require revolutionary thinking to create the new solution. Other times, opportunity is found by applying an old solution to a new problem. Other times a new solution is applied to an old problem. The Next Normal requires a flexibility in strategy.

While working with leaders in real estate, sales, and business, Total Career Growth observes many coaches and training programs that insist there is one "Secret Sauce" method of success. They insist that an individual will succeed if they simply follow the prescribed, proven program. "All you need to do is to follow these steps."

Pat Lynch, my business and podcast partner, and I agree that if you follow one of those programs, you are likely to be successful. That is, if conditions remain the same. If everything remains the same as the individual who achieved the success and created the program, then you should succeed. That makes senses. At that point, the only variable is you and your performance. If the process works for you, great!

But, what if it doesn't? That's a big IF. If the process doesn't' work, if you don't make enough sales or climb the ladder, the creator of the program assumes it is your fault. After all, it worked for them and many others. The program is a proven success so you must have failed at some point. The only way it failed was that you didn't follow the process as prescribed.

Granted, if you didn't follow the process as prescribed, then you share some of the blame.

But ask the crazy question, "What if it wasn't my fault?"

**Why Best Practices Fail**

There are three reasons why best practices or proven programs don't work.

First, our culture has changed. As I write this, we believe the end of the pandemic is in sight. The hope we feel today is better than it was last summer when the virus was spreading uncontrollably. Businesses have collapsed while the virtual world has expanded. We have learned to work and play virtually. More Baby Boomers have retired while Gen X are leading while Millennials and Gen Z find their place, creating new businesses and cultural trends. We have also changed as a culture with political polarization and racial sensitivity. Some opportunities have vanished while many others quickly appeared. In the process, the world has pivoted quickly into the Next Normal.

We need to look no further than the political polarization to notice how drastically the world has changed over the last few decades. Politicians have increasingly had to play to their base instead of work in a bipartisan manner to solve significant problems. Ideology has trumped pragmatism, science, tradition, and authority. The very way politicians communicate has shifted into the Next Normal. The questions aren't whether this is right or wrong as much as how we deal with it. If we don't become pivotal, purposely swiveling our focus to find the opportunities, we will be the antiquated leader.

That's not to say that we acquiesce or give up on our principles. Instead, my point is that the landscape has changed, and we will find the opportunities when we see the current and future world as it appears, not as we once saw it in the past.

That's where we can ask the crazy question. Looking at the radical changes, "What would happen if I did . . .?"

Second, we have changed as individuals. We are not the same people as we were before the latest shift. Look back and see how we changed following the Great Recession, terrorist attacks of 2001, Vietnam, the 1960s, or even World War II. Each of those events changed the people who lived through them. They changed us collectively and individually, as leaders and followers. Our business practices, buying habits, and service expectations changed.

Seeing how people have changed, this is the time to forecast the opportunities in the Next Normal. "What would happen if I . . . ?"

Third, and closely related to the two previous points, our customer pain has changed. We expect something different from the people we patronize. We aren't willing to wait as long or to tolerate as much. We are more self-centered yet more conscious of suffering whether it be human, animal, or environmental. There is a growing intolerance of insensitivity.

So, what happens if we ask that crazy question like Mahlum did when she noticed the homeless while she was running. "I wonder what would happen if I . . . ?" It was her ability to connect with their pain that motivated her. It wasn't just a matter of "what" or "how" but rather connecting with the "why?" Simon Sinek was right. Once you know their why, you can determine what and how.

Ask another crazy question, "Is it time to reconsider best practices and proven programs?"

**The Crazy Question in Brainstorming Solutions**

Anyone who is experienced in brainstorming knows that the crazy, far out freaky question probably isn't the solution, but it opens the door to the solution. The crazy question expands our thinking so we can consider what we dismissed as "IMPOSSIBLE."

The Apollo 13 crew faced a dire situation that NASA hadn't experienced before. They couldn't skip the problem. To make matters worse, their resources and energy were limited, complicating the problem solution to create a solution. Their solution came when astronauts on the ground worked with others to create a solution. At times, they must have felt like it was impossible, and the crew was doomed.

In the end, the solution required asking crazy questions such as looking at an ordinary or out of place item and wondering, "Will this work?"

That's how 3M created sticky notes. The failed glue project became an extraordinarily successful new product.

How does this apply to strategy? Strategy is the series of actions one takes to make a dream a reality. The Next Normal demands more flexibility in creating that strategy.

Are you willing to ask the crazy question to:
- Find the opportunity?
- Create your team?
- Build your processes?
- Design your action plan?
- Solve problems quickly?
- Outmaneuver the competition?
- Collaborate to expand your market?
- Scale your business?

**Ask the Crazy Question**

As leaders in all areas of business, government, and civic arenas, this is the time to ask the crazy questions.

Ask the crazy question about their why. "I wonder why this is so important?" "I wonder what motivates them?"

Ask the crazy question about innovative ways to solve their problem. "What new resources are out there that I'm not familiar with?" "I wonder what other resources we already have that could be used to solve this new problem?"

Ask yourself the crazy question. It might be phrased in a couple different ways. Either way, think outside that cliché box.

"What would I like to do that I never thought possible?"

"What would happen if I or we did . . .?"

Ask the absurd question. Don't dismiss it. Say it out loud. Write it down. Challenge yourself to see if it really is that crazy.

That's the insight Pivotal Leaders use to do what others never thought possible.

Rest assured, there is not only one solution to the seemingly impossible problem of the Next Normal. There are more opportunities than you can imagine. Most of them are at your fingertips when you are willing to ask the crazy question.

**Your Challenge**

Don't listen to the critics. Identify the pain. Identify their why and use that to determine your strategy.

In the process, it might just work. If not, it is likely get you thinking in a way that leads to the viable solution.

After all, it worked for Anne Mahlum.

What do you think? Does that sound crazy?

## 12: FOSTER DISRUPTION

Pivotal Leadership fosters disruptive innovation. Leading disruption is a mindset, a pattern of thinking, and a habit. Becoming a disruptive thinker is a paradigm shift that becomes a lifestyle, not simply a one-time experience.

The challenge for most people is that they are so used to complying with the rules that they cannot imagine asking the crazy question. They can't imagine breaking rules without feeling guilty or worrying about getting in trouble. That's because we've been conditioned for stability, not change.

Obedience provides a safety net for followers afraid to innovate. Followers, in other words, those that are not innovators, will only try something new if someone provides a safe place to fail.

Think about that.

Obedient people will not try anything new if there is a high risk of failure, embarrassment, and consequences. If, however, there is a way to protect their position, reputation, and pride, then they are more willing to explore. Granted, some are so unwilling to extend the effort to do anything to change their comfort zone and status quo.

Pivotal Leaders hone a different mindset. They are "different animals" because they are incredibly focused on future opportunities. They purposely push themselves out of their comfort zone, the status quo, and successes from the past. They focus on opportunity, not the potential failure. That focus is radically different from followers, managers, and positional leaders.

## Richard Branson

Richard Branson is known for his bold approach to business. He is willing to tackle industry giants like British Airways and some of the world's most devastating social problems. He is known to say that he doesn't enter any business venture unless he can disrupt that industry.

He provides wise advice. "If someone offers you an amazing opportunity and you're not sure you can do it, say yes- then learn how to do it later."

That is a radical divergence from what most of us have been taught. Instead of playing it safe, he believes in accepting the challenge and then figuring out how to do it.

In other words, don't wait.

That is bold mindset. Notice three qualities that foster that disruptive mindset.

## Urgency

Branson's approach illustrates a strong sense of urgency that waits for no one or anything. It shows the brevity of opportunity and how quickly we must respond less it disappears.

Disruptive leaders are not patient when pursuing breakthrough opportunities. They are not impatient in a way that they make rash decisions either. Instead, they are driven with a resolve to seize this opportunity. It gets them up in the morning and keeps them up at night. Urgency is a driving factor that compels them to do what others don't, won't, or can't because they don't have the incentive. Disruptive leaders work with the determination to finish.

Urgency becomes part of the Pivotal Leader's being, a mindset that they embrace, a way of thinking derived from the paradigm shift to the future. It becomes who they are. Remember, it doesn't mean they are rashly impatient but rather unwilling to quit or to settle.

*PIVOTAL LEADERS*

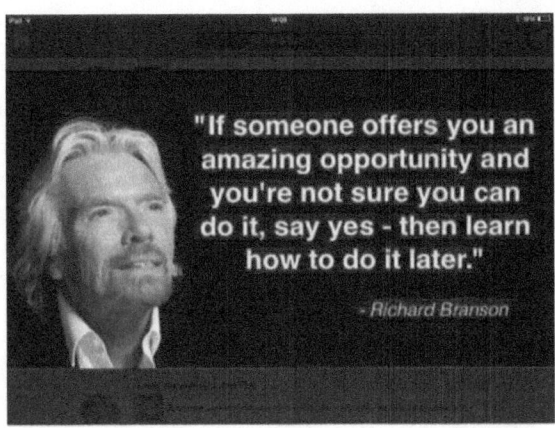

### Flexibility

Notice the willingness to adapt in Branson's quote. He commits to the goal and is willing to do whatever he needs to learn how to do it. The method is flexible, but the goal is not.

Flexibility implies an ability and willingness to bend. It is the opposite of ridged. Too often when followers see an opportunity, they say, "Unfortunately I cannot . . . or I am not . . ." Notice the rigidity. Also notice that the rigidity dictates the end result, a failure. They cannot succeed because of something they believe they cannot do. Instead, Branson's comment illustrates how we can succeed when we are willing to learn and become what we need to succeed.

Rigidity says, "I cannot not" as if fate, DNA, and the universe have dictated our future. Flexibility, however, asks, "What if I . . .? Why not?" Pivotal Leaders don't accept the answers the world claims but instead asks the critical questions to do what others have already determined are impossible. They are flexible to the outcomes and the methods of achieving that success.

Notice what happens when we foster that flexible mindset. Notice our willingness to explore, learn, and grow. Then notice the results that follow.

Flexibility fosters a mindset that says, "Yeah, let's do it."

### Confidence

You can imagine how that fosters disruption by way of a personal confidence. Gone is the debilitating fear, replaced with a bold confidence that the opportunity is within reach. It is NOT too big for us.

I like that – and I'm not one of those overly confident people from birth. In fact, I suffered from a lack of confidence for years. I like this mindset because it shows that confidence is a way of thinking that can be learned based on our past successes as well as our hope for the future. The negative past does not have to repeat itself.

**Destiny**

Doubt and failure is not our destiny. Instead, we determine our own destiny based on the confidence, flexibility, and urgency we take into business and life. In the end, confidence is a choice, an attitude we choose to develop, not a curse that crushes our dreams. Disruptive leaders foster change and growth. They are willing to be flexible to pursue opportunities with confidence.

**Your Challenge**

Notice this mindset is a choice. It is not dictated by DNA, fate, or the universe.

Does your mindset reflect urgency, flexibility, and confidence?

Foster disruption to seize the best opportunities in the Next Normal.

## 13: RETHINK REJECTION & FAILURE

Pivoting to the Next Normal requires the right mindset. That requires re-thinking rejection and failure.

**Blame and Shame**

Many people don't think. They react emotionally. To think is to "to employ one's mind rationally and objectively in evaluating or dealing with a given situation. (Dictionary.com) Notice it requires using rationally and objectivity.

Rationality eliminates blame.

Objectivity eliminates shame.

Notice that rejection and failure are saturated with emotional blame and shame. Failure indicates you did something wrong. It blames you for at least part of the results. Rejection takes blame farther. Not only are you to blame, but you are also a bad person that needs to be rejected, excluded from the group. Blame can be objective, but shame is subjective. It becomes very personal.

That's why I coach my clients to eliminate the word "shame" from their vocabulary. There is no justified reason for using it. Good people make mistakes. Sometimes good people make big mistakes. That is no reason to shame them.

When we operate out of either blame or shame, we are reacting emotionally, not thinking. We are definitely not thinking strategically, collaboratively, or compassionately.

**Thinking**

Thinking is the opposite of emotional reaction. It involves using logic to piece together evidence in a way that objectively leads to a conclusion. Thinking is driven by facts, not feelings or opinions.

To pivot to the next normal, leaders must look beyond their negative emotions to see the objective facts. Failing to look beyond negative emotions leaves one paralyzed in the Old Normal and miss the phenomenal Next Normal opportunities.

That requires a pivot in our mindset, from emotional reaction to logical thinking. To pivot and create pivotal teams, leaders must foster the ability to rise above the emotions and engage minds. That requires rethinking failure. a

**Fear of Rejection**

Jia Jiang is a disruptive leader who pushes himself beyond the pain of rejection. Being frustrated with his ability in sales, he knew he had to become more resilient. So, he challenged himself to 100 days of rejection. Each day he purposely challenged himself to ask a stranger for something. He thought that by hearing "No" for 100 straight days that he would desensitize himself to rejection.

Notice how he welcomed failure to help him succeed where he hadn't before. He identified his pain in failure. He recognized his "why" and strategized his "how" to get to his ultimate "what."

This is a strange method of self-compassion. To help alleviate his own pain, he worked to inoculate himself by overcoming one small pain at a time.

The pain of past and potential failures haunts most of us. Too often it paralyses us to the point of avoiding potentially great opportunities.

No wonder so many struggle with the fear of rejection. They believe that rejection is the ultimate stamp on their flaws and fate dictates their destiny. Once rejected, the end of the story is written.

But disruptive leaders know rejection is simply one of the many twists in life's adventure. To succeed in doing what others consider "impossible." They learn to do what others won't, don't, or can't. When someone tells them "No," they move on to the next person.

Jia Jiang, feeling frustrated by his fear of failure, scratched out 100 challenges. He started by asking a stranger for $100. I wonder how many of us would have chosen that as our first day challenge. Wasn't there be something easier? After all, wouldn't he want to start building his confidence with a success? With all the trepidation you would expect, he walked up to a stranger and blurted out his request. Oddly enough, the stranger didn't quickly dismiss him, but simply said, "Why?" Jiang was too nervous and fearing rejection to give him an answer, primarily because he hadn't thought that far. So, he quickly turned and ran away. Only later did he realize that people are much more willing to say "yes" than what he imagined.

Over the next 99 days he asked a variety of crazy questions such as, "Can I have a burger refill?" or "can I plant a flower in your yard?" As he progressed, he didn't just desensitize himself to rejection, he learned how to ask in a way that he didn't get rejected. He learned to succeed. Imagine what that did for his sales abilities.

Disruptive leaders face their fears while followers allow their fears to dictate their future. The old scripture says conveys a modern lesson, "You don't have because you don't ask."

**Your Challenge**

Are you asking for what you want or need?

Or are you silent because you have already decided the answer?

What if you are wrong? What will happen when you find people are more willing to help you than instantly hurt you.

Then ask yourself, "How can I change the way I ask to make it easier for them to say yes?"

Rethinking rejection and failure leads to creating a cutting-edge attitude.

# 14: CREATE A CUTTING-EDGE ATTITUDE

To do what no one has done before, your team needs a cutting-edge attitude. That begins with the leader, you, believing so much in yourself, that you refuse to apologize for being pivotal. As Mellody Hobson, President and co-CEO of Ariel Investments, said on the Adam Grant podcast, Worklife, "I'm unapologetically black." He also noted that she was unapologetically a woman. She owns her ethnicity even when others question or dismiss it.

In the same way, pivotal leaders are willing to stand boldly in the face of doubt and criticism and defend their pivotal perspective and calling. As a pivotal leader myself, many will push back wondering, "Why can't you just go along?" I'm not going to apologize for settling for substandard results. I won't settle in my personal life nor will I settle for those organizations that seek my input.

Being unapologetic, as Hobson noted, is being kind but not soft, strong but not tough, nonthreatening but not threatened. The pivotal attitude is not meant to hurt but does make many uncomfortable. Those that are comfortable, or demanding to be safe at all times, or needing predictability at every turn will be uncomfortable with your pivotal attitude.

To navigate the treacherous waters into the Next Normal, we need a belief that "I can do it. Just watch me." We also need an attitude that says, "I'm sorry if you are uncomfortable, but this needs to happen, or we will suffer later." It's not a personal threat or an ego trip. It is the prophet tracking the trends and forecasting the opportunities. Some may see it as a swaggering confidence on the verge of arrogance with a hint of defiance. That is their fear emerging. Don't be derailed from the pivot because of their fears.

We all recognize a defiant, destructive attitude where a child or adult purposely destroys something. In a future book I discuss Audacious Success. Audacious is often seen as "over the line" or "reckless." Change that focus from destructive to constructive and we start to see the attitude necessary for innovation.

How can you develop that attitude?

How can you create that attitude in your team?

**Cutting-Edge Attitude**

I love the attitude of the woman in the photo. She displays all three parts of a pivotal, cutting-edge attitude, according to the ABC Model of Attitudes.

**A – Affective**

Our attitude about change and disruption is marked by a feeling. It likely terrifies many who want to play it safe and maintain the Old Normal. However, a cutting-edge attitude is invigorated with innovation and radical change. When we have this position, we feel good about what we are going to make happen. Good feelings are critical as they provide the emotional anchor that ties us to our future. Bad feelings also serve as an anchor, only to the Old Normal. Without that anchor to the New Normal, we often retreat in the presence of incredible opportunities.

But let's face it. There are a lot of things that frighten us about the future.

- How will A.I. displace workers?
- Is global warming real?
- How soon will it affect us?
- Will the mass shootings continue?
- Will the pandemic return?
- Will the economy tank again?
- If so, what will the future look like?

Each of us have a variety of fears. But remember, fears are often unfounded. Analyze them and you will expose the lies. Nevertheless, fear paralyzes many when it comes to disruptive opportunities.

To work through our fears, ask the following questions:
- How do you feel when we talk about disruptive change? (Be honest.)
- How does your team feel when you discuss your innovative vision? (Don't assume, listen to them.)
- How can I use reason to work through those irrational fears?

## B – Behavioral

Many people allow fear to paralyze them. They have incredible opportunities available to them but freeze in their tracks. They can't step into the Next Normal because they are clinging to the Old Normal. It's not just fear, it has a noticeable effect.

Now consider that risk taking individual who steps forward and says, "I'll try it." Notice how others react to our bold behavior. Notice how others join the leader. Now notice how that behavior melts the fears of both leaders and followers.

We have all seen it in the horror movies. Something terrifying happens, the characters freeze, giving opportunity for the villain to attack.

Also notice that some respond, "I couldn't help myself. I was afraid." They refused to change their behavior because of their fears.

*"If you're going through hell keep going."*
Winston Churchill

Winston Churchill's quote says it well, "If you're going through hell keep going." You may feel like stopping but do the opposite.

Too often people create habits (repeated, unconscious behaviors) from what they have felt was right before. Too often we behave based on a perceived fear that we believe might happen. Doesn't that sound silly when you read it say it aloud?

Monitor your behavior. Watch for behaviors that are based on our fears, not on the potential of an opportunity.

People often resist changing behaviors.

What behavior does your team foster toward your innovative vision?

What behavior do you take to foster that cutting-edge mindset?

**C-Cognitive**

A cutting-edge pivotal attitude thinks much bigger than the ordinary, obedient follower. Pivotal leaders pause to say, "I wonder what would happen if we did . . .?" They think about ideas and opportunities that others ignore. When followers are content with the ordinary, they are seeing potential for the ultimate. When those followers dismiss the potential by asking, "Why?" the respond with, "Why not?"

Part of the problem with the ordinary follower thinking is that they are not using the neocortex part of the brain. Instead, of that logical, problem solving portion, they revert through the ruts in their brain to the emotional center in the amygdala. They emotionally react instead of logically process.

Until we train our brains, most of us are conditioned to react based on impulse. Instead, once we have reprogramed our brain to prioritize the logical, the emotional rules, especially in surprise situations.

For example, what do you think when a serious problem erupts? Do you have a moment of panic? Does that moment last much longer?

Let's try another example. How do you react, be honest, when an executive breaks the news of a major disruption in the organization? This could be a massive shift in structure or even layoffs?

Many freeze, unable or refusing to think their way through it. Unless someone rescues them, their fate is sealed. Pivotal leaders play the Superhero role of their own disruption.

This last part is critical. If you follow me on social media or have read any of my previous books, you know that my focus is helping you to think bigger so you can reach higher. Disruptive innovation is fostered when we as leaders are brave enough to challenge our own thinking, beliefs, and values.

Too many settle for ordinary results instead of reaching for the ultimate because they are afraid of failure. We call that "risk averse."

But think about it. If we are afraid (have negative feelings) of failure, we will only change (behavioral) if we believe (think) we will succeed. That seems like a wise business decision.

But again, think about it. How often do those "can't miss" opportunities arise? Is there ever a "no fail" opportunity? Of course not. As pivotal, disruptive leaders, our challenge is to minimize the risks by gathering the best information and team to ensure our success. Take the strategic action because we believe in the opportunity. (Affective, Behavioral and Cognitive).

**Your Challenge**

The challenge is to build that cutting-edge team that welcomes the opportunity to do what others never thought possible.

What do you think about radical change and disruptive opportunities?

How can you reach higher by transforming your own thinking?

How can you help your team overcome their fear of failure?

In the end, are you unashamedly a pivotal leader? If so, you will display two specific attitudes that ordinary followers might claim is rude.

First, you will be wisely impatient. Having tracked the trends and forecasting the opportunities, you will be driven by an urgency for acting at the perfect time. When the opportunity is ripe, there is no time to wait. That doesn't mean you recklessly act before the time is right. Wisely impatient is a disciplined urgency.

Second, you become intolerant of those unwilling to think bigger and reach higher. You can't tolerate ordinary goals and reach the ultimate. There is no way you can be a pivotal leader by resisting valuable change. Instead, you exude the pivotal mindset. That is who you are at your core, and it radiates from your pores.

Notice how each of these two will alienate you from smaller thinkers and hesitant reactors. While you are not rude, a pivotal attitude that separates you from those spectators. Many will criticize in an attempt to keep you from getting too far ahead. That doesn't matter to you. To do what you ultimate want to do, you must pivot to think bigger and reach higher.

## 15: FOSTER FLEXIBILITY

Innovation thrives on flexibility. Unfortunately, that is the last thing most organizations welcome.

A friend of mine, Eric Wilson, is the medical massage therapist I mentioned earlier. He specializes in Active Isolated Stretching. By working with him over the last 15 years, I have done far more than I ever thought possible.

**Thinking Bigger**

I was in my 50s when my wife suggested we run a 5K. Her office was putting together teams for the local Gasparilla race. She developed asthma in her 20s and was told by her doctor that she would never run again. Although she wasn't a runner at that time, she begrudgingly accepted his diagnosis and prognosis. Three decades later, she asked the crazy question, "Why not try to run?" That's when she came home and asked if I wanted to join her. That wasn't such a crazy question as I had jogged for fitness in my 30s but hadn't continued.

She went online and found a "Couch to 5K" program and we started training. We ran the 5K and then quit until training for the race the following year. Along the way, we asked another not so crazy question, "What if we ran another local race to train for Gasparilla?" By the fourth year, we were training year around and enjoying the process. That's when I asked another seemingly crazy question in the form of a statement. "I want to see how far and how fast I can run."

Granted by that time, I was in my upper 50s and well past my prime. I knew I wouldn't win any race unless there was no one else running. But I stretched my thinking from "I'm getting old" to "How fast and far can I run?" Over the next three years we progressed to run 15Ks and then half marathons.

My wife had gone along with my bigger thinking until I mentioned the word, "marathon" without a half before it. "No" was the immediate response. But as she became comfortable with training and running for a half marathon, we reluctantly agreed to sing up for a full marathon in 2018.

Notice how each step required thinking bigger. We weren't natural runners. We still don't enjoy running as many do. It is not our sanctuary where we can't wait to get out the door and in our own world. Instead, we push ourselves to do what we never thought we would do.

How was that flexibility important to seizing Next Normal opportunities? Why is flexibility so important to your innovation?

## The Winning Trifecta

Everyone knows that to run a marathon requires extensive training. and the proper fuel. You just don't get off the couch and run 26.2 miles. Everyone knows that.

Strengthening muscles takes time. We consulted a running coach about our progress, moving toward the marathon. They agreed that our 3-year plan to move from 10Ks to a full marathon was wise, especially given our age. It could be done quicker but we wanted to ensure we strengthened our muscles and mindset at the right pace. Even now, as established runners, we know that to train for a half marathon takes about 2 months of focused work. A full marathon takes 4 months. We follow the advice to only increase our mileage about 10% a week.

But the savvy, experienced runner understands that strengthening the muscles is only half of the process. Stretching those muscles is just as important to keep them pliable and free of injury. Injury stops us in our tracks, sidelines us for weeks if not months, and threatens to curtail our potential and progress. It is damage to our bodies and a setback to our hopes and dreams. Injury frustrates our success.

In business, many of our organizations focus heavily upon strength, demanding that we become lean and mean. Some are good at providing the training, but many fall short. Still others recognize the requirements to continue their progress (beyond a paycheck.) Very few recognize the importance of stretching the mindset or developing the flexibility to create disruptive innovation.

## Inflexible Signs

A runner can tell when their muscles are tight. They feel resistance instead of pliability. In the same way, innovative leaders recognize resistance in their own thinking and in their team. They hone their sensitivity to seeing and hearing the signs of inflexibility. They listen for the following comments:
- "I'm not sure about that."
- "I've never done it that way before."
- "That's not the way I like to do it."
- "I found my way works better."
- "That's not our tradition/culture.
- "It's too hard."
- "You have to understand, ..."

Notice that these comments reflect a fear of change. The individual or the group are not confident the new method will be successful. They also don't know what they are capable of. No wonder they are afraid of trying.

Challenge yourself with the crazy question. "What is your team afraid of when facing innovative opportunities?"

## Deflect the Criticism

When my wife and I first started running, we received three snarky comments that we have used as motivation.
- "Why would you want to do that? "
- "Are you trying to develop a bad heart or bad knees?"
- "If you see me running, call the cops because someone is chasing me."

Critics are not there to help but to prove their point. They deflect the innovative opportunity based on a direct challenge, explaining their defense, or trying to be funny. Notice in their humor, they are creating a thick wall of protection, so they don't feel guilty about denying the opportunity.

Ask the crazy question, "What challenges are you receiving from your critics?"

## Counter the Excuses

As we have encouraged others to get out and move to feel better and be healthier, we have heard a number of excuses (which are simply inflexible thoughts coming out."

- "I don't like to run."
- "I can't run."
- "It's too much work."
- "I'm too busy."
- "I have kids."
- "You have to understand . . ."

Inflexibility is the excuse of those unwilling to disrupt the present for the great opportunities of the future. Listen for the inflexibility and offer an opportunity to stretch their thinking.

What excuses are you hearing about their flexibility?

Are you using any of those excuses for your own inflexibility?

Hear that flexibility as fear of change. They just don't understand what is possible.

## Offer a Different Perspective

While training for our marathon, we adopted a run-walk-run system that has worked well. Like many runners, we thought the only way to be an authentic runner was to start running a race and not stop to walk. We struggled to make it beyond a 10k with that method. So we adopted the Jeff Galloway system that was a radical change.

The system we use is to run 30 seconds, walk 30 seconds and repeat the cycle. At times we will shift to a 15-30 system.

We used this system when we ran our first marathon in January of 2018. We continue to use it because it makes a seemingly impossible venture a reality.

What new system can you offer your team that makes what they thought was "impossible" a reality?

### Make Flexibility Easy

I have explained the system to many people who are amazed that if you run for 15 seconds and walk for 30 then repeat the cycle, you can finish a half marathon in about 3 hours 15 minutes. You can finish a full marathon in 6 hours 30 minutes. We know we because we just ran a half marathon in 3 hours and 1 minute using the 15-30 (We had a good pace that day.)

The response often is "I can do that!" Who can't? Almost everyone can run for 15 seconds.

How can you show your team how easy it is to be flexible?

### Find Your Reward

We also say, "We don't love running." That is the truth. Running is a chore and not something that we welcome. But we do it for the results we desire. We run to challenge ourselves, receive the finisher medals, and accolades from those that appreciate our accomplishments.

What reward does your team need to become more flexible?

### Great Stories Encourage Flexibility

My wife and I like to tell people how much fun it is to connect with others while running. I recently met a woman that is about 70 years old who has walked 72 half marathons. She doesn't run or pretend to. She simply walks. That is impressive. I know it makes me want to keep going.

We have met another of others, like Aaron Burros who is in the process of achieving his audacious goal of running the world's 6 greatest major marathons and then running 50 marathons in 50 states in 50 weeks although he suffers from PTSD and has 2 bullet fragments in his body. But maybe what is most impressive about Aaron is his energy. He was my pacer for a 15K and he made it the most enjoyable run I have experienced. Everyone on the course heard us singing, laughing, and shouting. I wish he was my pacer for every race.

Each of those individuals provide great stories of inspiration. While running the Lincoln, Nebraska half marathon, we were approximately halfway through the race when we heard this rhythmic scraping sound behind us. Gradually it got closer. As he passed, we saw a former military member running on two artificial legs. We thought, "If he can run after suffering those injuries, I have no complaints." We instantly had more energy and that propelled us through the rest of the race. We still think about him when we are tempted to complain.

What great, authentic stories inspire your team?

What stories help them to become more flexible?

How can you provide the energy to increase your team's flexibility?

**Supportive Systems**

Innovative organizations find systems that work for them. However, as you will see below, innovative organizations foster flexibility in their systems.

- Listen to the inflexibility.
- Offer a different perspective that works.
- Make it easy to be flexible.
- Find your reward (and theirs).
- Tell great, but true, stories of innovation.

Flexibility is critical to pivot to your Next Normal success. But are you flexible enough to break the rules and survive?

**Your Challenge**

In what ways are you inflexible?

How is that rigidity causing frustration and pain for you and your team?

## 16: BREAK THE RULES

Rules are fascinating aspects of life. They serve a purpose but sometimes, we need to break those rules to pivot to the next great opportunity.

For example, the Merriam-Webster dictionary provides the following definitions.
- a prescribed guide for conduct or action.
- laws or regulations prescribed by the founder of a religious order for observance by its members.
- an accepted procedure, custom, or habit.
- a usually written order or direction made by a court regulating court practice or the action of parties.
- a legal precept or doctrine.
- a regulation or bylaw governing procedure or controlling conduct.
- a usually valid generalization.
- a generally prevailing quality, state, or mode.
- a standard of judgment: criterion.
- a regulating principle.

- a determinate method for performing a mathematical operation and obtaining a certain result.
- the exercise of authority or control: dominion.
- a period during which a specified ruler or government exercises control.
- a strip of material marked off in units used especially for measuring:

Notice that rules are prescribed, habit, written, legal, generalized, used for judgment, regulating, authoritative, and practical. Without rules, life would be a chaotic collision of individual desires, organizational dysfunction, and continual, unnecessary re-invention. Rules make our lives and business better because they provide order, predictability, and stability. In other words, rules are exceptionally valuable to society.

Order and stability are particularly valuable during disruptions. Traumas are tough times that suddenly throw us into turmoil, leaving us numb, confused, and demoralized. We don't know what happened or how to proceed. Our window to the world has been shattered and we stand bruised and bloody. In those times when life shatters around us, we need some semblance of order to find our safety and regain our composure.

So why would we want to break the rules?

**Tough Times**

Rules are made for certain situations. They are times when good rules, taken too far, harm rather than help. Civil disobedience may be necessary to correct a bureaucratic nightmare. Rules applied broadly often hurt the people intended to help. Can you imagine never outgrowing your 8:00 p.m. bedtime began as a toddler? Sometimes rules need to be changed. Other times, they need to be broken.

To change a rule implies that the same set of authorities that set the rules are openminded and willing to adapt to the changing environment. But what if those authorities don't see a need for change? As a regulation and as an exercise of authority, the rule stays in place. That's when the individual is faced with a severe choice: obey or disobey. Obedience keeps them in the good graces of the authorities and community. Disobedience may provide individual satisfaction but bring community scrutiny.

But what happens when life breaks our rules? We all have established rules for our lives to bring stability, predictability, and happiness. We have established what we believe and value. We have honed the processes that make our lives better, faster, cheaper, easier, and more enjoyable. We have settled into a safe world that we have carefully constructed. How do we reinvent that safe world?

Tough Times shatter our world. As we have discussed earlier, Tough Times are anything that disrupts our comfort zone. They might be slight inconveniences or life altering traumas. They can be a shift in management, governmental regulations, the economy. Tough Times may also mean pay cuts, layoffs, or industry extinction. On a personal level, Tough Times can be traumatic with the loss of a limb or loved one. Tough Times change the rules of what we think is fair, right or expected. They shatter our stability, customs, and control. We have no other choice but to live in that new world.

At that point, we must make new rules to go forward. We have all lost jobs and loved ones. Life gives us no choice; we must go forward without them. To do so requires that we adopt at least one new rule.

**Innovation**

Then there are times where life is too stable and predictable. Life is boring. We need some energy, so we shock our world by breaking one of the rules. It may be a rule set by others or one that we have established ourselves for another time. Breaking these rules is like choosing to remodel your home, busting down a wall and changing the floorplan.

During the 2020 pandemic, favorite restaurants were shut down and travel restricted. While that was traumatic for some, it was the perfect opportunity for others. Many chose to clean out their closets and remodel their homes. Others remodeled their lives, learning how to cook or a new language. They broke their old rules to find novelty, which is simply their Next Normal for enjoyment.

Others saw the shutdown as an opportunity to capitalize and ramp up their business. Zoom exploded and other platforms quickly followed. Professional speakers quickly pivoted to offering online speeches and courses. Musicians held online concerts. Restaurants provided curbside pickup and delivery. Museums provided online tours. Wineries provided virtual tastings. To survive or to find new ways to live, we innovate during Tough Times. That is our pivot or breakthrough into the Next Normal.

Is it time for you to break the rules?

## What rules need to be broken?

I'm not a rebel. I don't defy authority because I want my own way or hate obeying. Instead, I find life goes better when everyone follows the rules. But when it comes to doing what we have never done before, I find that the rules often hold us back. That can't happen if we are serious about disruptive innovation.

It Starts with Rules – Breaking Them!

I must admit, I'm conflicted by saying that. For most of my life, I've followed the rules. That all changed when I found that many of the rules did more harm than good. That made me stop and think. "Why am I following rules that do more harm than good? It was when I started ignoring and breaking the rules that I started seeing innovative success.

Please understand, the rules I'm addressing here are ones that don't hurt or endanger anyone. Instead, the rules that I find do more harm than good are set by people merely to benefit themselves. They may not even been created to favor someone but now someone is enforcing them for that purpose. In other words, those rules are unjust and I'm not benefiting from them.

The innovator knows which rules to break. For example, Elon Musk broke the rules established by automobile manufactures that required cars to be sold through dealerships. Musk, thinking like an entrepreneur, recognized the value of selling directly to the consumer. He found a way to circumvent the law so I can now buy one through the Tesla store at the mall.

Part of Albert Einstein's genius was knowing which laws to break. Thorpe (2000) detailed how to break out of this "rule rut." Great ideas lie just outside of our prevailing thought. Otherwise, someone would have found them already. You must break the rules to solve impossible problems." (p.5. *How to Think Like Einstein*.)

Are you bold enough to re-examine the rules?
Are you bold enough to break them?

Are you wise enough to know which rules to break?
For many, that is a radical move for three reasons.

**First, we all break the rules for the wrong reason.**

There are those that break the rules because they don't want to follow them. They are the anarchists, rebels, or malcontents that make life difficult for others and enjoy it. They are destructive, not disruptive.

Sometimes we are those destructive people. We tear down to reinforce our fragile ego. Other times we disobey to prove someone wrong, tear down their ego, or prove a point. Sometimes, as with the speed limit, we break the rules because it is too inconvenient or uncomfortable.

The problem comes in that we are not making something better. We just want to do it our way. That is enjoyable but not productive. Often that causes unnecessary problems.

If you want to breakthrough, maybe it is time you started breaking some of the rules for the right reasons.
- Do you have a protocol for breaking rules in order to innovate?
- Do you punish those who want to innovate and break a rule? Which Rules?

**Second, we break the wrong rules.**

Einstein didn't break all the rules. He knew which rules he had to break to find his breakthrough. The challenge for any innovative leader is to understand which rules need to be obeyed and which ones need to be broken. That discernment is where many make their critical mistakes and miss great opportunities.

For example, the modern trend while remodeling a home removes walls to create an open floor plan. However, the contract quickly determines which wall is supporting the structure. Some walls simply close in a room while others support the upper floors and rafters. The contract knows that if changes are to be made to the load bearing wall, significant reinforcement must be made.

What rules cannot be broken without significant consequences?

This principle was tested during the pandemic. As mentioned before, many organizations demanded "butts in seats" as a measure of productivity prior to the pandemic. They adhered to that rule believing that the structure of their organization would collapse if violated. But when they were forced to work virtually, they realized that wasn't a load bearing wall as they thought. Instead, productivity is that rule that supports the structure. They found that productivity can be ensured in other ways. That rule can be broken without significant consequences.

Which rules have you refused to break for fear of considerable consequences?

Which of those rules proved they could be broken?

Which ones are you willing to test?

**Third, we break the rules in the wrong way.**

Compliance is the easiest and often the only way to survive. Unfortunately, compliance kills creativity. After all, organizations work best when there is a clear process for operation. Yet there is seldom a process for breaking the rules. It is so far outside the boundaries of an organizational strategy that they haven't created a process for it. Is there any wonder why they don't foster a cutting-edge culture?

One of the best ways to break a rule is to ignore it. You don't have to say or do anything. You just simply go about your business.

Another way is the opposite, you tell people what is wrong, and you are actively working to break that rule.

Somewhere in between is a quiet resolution that you will change it.

**Banksy**

Artists have been known for redesigning the box for centuries. But Banksy and other graffiti arts have taken it to a new level by ignoring public rules.

You might recognize the artwork below by Banksy that became the most appreciated art in all of Great Britain in 2017.

**How did they break the rules?**

First, instead of using the conventional private space, they utilize public walls. It is called graffiti and dismissed by many because the rules dictate that one cannot deface public or private property. They didn't ask permission and that rankles many. However, that was the way to get their art noticed. They didn't have the means to garner a private art show, so they took it public. This illegal exposure ultimately brought them attention and appreciation for their skill and message.

Notice that they knew which rules to ignore. Innovative organizations have very few rules because they understand creative individuals need the freedom to work "outside the box" and to redesign the box. The blank urban wall became their canvas.

In the same way, the old rule says you need a brick-and-mortar store. Modern rules say you need a website. Other rules say you need a live audience. Yet YouTube.com has shattered those rules. Where can you do business? What rules do you need to break to make that happen?

**Girl with Balloon by Banksy**

Second, the "graffiti" artists also defy social rules and take on controversial issues that polite society or politically correct factions won't condone. Banksy and his cohorts often criticize political actions, war, greed and even animal rights. They break the rules to start a discussion that helps others see the world in a new way. While that is often considered progressive, even those artists challenge the progressive viewpoint. It seems that as soon as the rule is created, they are breaking it. They keep pushing the boundaries with controversial issues.

What rules do you need to break about controversial issues?

Third, Banksy is fascinating because he has kept his identity a secret. That is breaking an old rule in business. The rule says, "Build your brand and make your money." "You don't want to be the best kept secret." But imagine the freedom that comes with voicing your messages in pictures and never having to constrict your subject matter.

That is a critical point.

There is an old saying that a person can do a great deal of good if they don't care who gets credit. The intriguing part is that the original author of that quote is unknown. Many claim the credit, as would be expected, but the true author has not been identified.

Which rules do you need to break about who gets credit?

### Which Rules will You Break?

Imagine fostering these three aspects of breaking rules in your organization. Imagine a team of passionate innovators willing to share the credit and make a significant difference. Imagine anonymous people raising controversial issues in public spaces. Imagine the chaos that would create.

Naturally, you aren't interested in breaking the rules simply to create confusion. Instead, imagine righting a social wrong, illuminating a better method, or creating a valuable product.

Imagine the next great idea. Imagine creating a process that fosters that innovative thinking, openly embracing the challenge that might just provide the desired breakthrough. Wouldn't that be worth the discomfort of someone breaking the rules?

### Your Challenge

We each have incredible opportunities in the rapidly and radically changing world. To realize the best opportunities, we must break the rules.
- Are you willing to break the rules?
- If so, which ones?
- Are you breaking those rules for the right reason?

# 17: OVERCOME ANY OBSTACLE

Any major shift in our work or life creates obstacles that we must overcome. Many of those need to be navigated quickly.

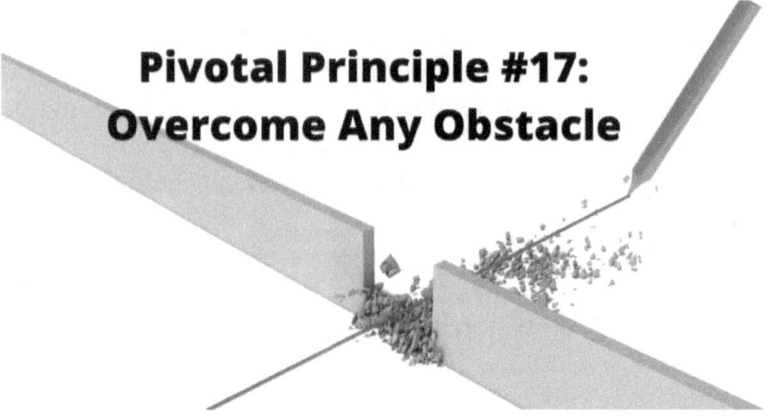

Remember when the pandemic shut us down in the spring of 2020. We were suddenly forced to learn how to work remotely, creating a virtual office for the first time. That created problems for both management and staff. By now, everyone has figured out how to overcome that obstacle. But there is another obstacle hidden within that virtual office challenge. To break the rules, we need to understand how to become comfortable in the Next Normal. We need to find our new comfort zone.

**First, Create Your Space.**

When I was a college professor, I enjoyed going to work and mingling with the faculty, students, and staff. I missed that when I left academia for the world of executive coaching and consulting. The first challenge was to not just create my physical space, but also each of my eight types of spaces: physical, financial, emotional, intellectual, career, social/recreational, family, and ethical/spiritual. Your Next Normal may not require disrupting each of those spaces. However, be prepared that your next Normal must become your new comfort zone in many areas of your life.

**Physical Space.**

Everyone will have their own unique ranking of these eight spaces. When I left academia, I started with the physical space. My wife and I were empty nesters, so we had a spare bedroom that I already used as my home office. That was an easy choice.

The biggest challenge for those used to working in a physical office is establishing a Next Normal physical space. It might be a coffee table or your favorite coffee shop, your laptop, or your car. It might not be a designated space at all. What's important is to know the rules.

Where can you work?

Where do you want to work?

Where do you do your best work?

Where can others find you when they need you?

If physical space is a priority, mark your territory by making an agreement with yourself and others. Like Sheldon Cooper on *The Big Bang* TV series, claim your spot. Make a new rule by setting the boundaries and enforcing them.

As a Pivotal Leader, you are challenged to determine the best place for your team to work. Can you be productive working remotely? Will you be more productive in a hybrid situation? Or was the old way of working together in one location the best way to innovate?

**Financial Space**

Where will you make money?

This is the critical point pivoting into the Next Normal for every business and employee. Layoffs and the threat of industry extinction challenge us in our financial space.

Ten years ago, I was working with the CEO of a small printing company. The industry was evaporating with the onset of digital marketing, and he was having difficulty pivoting. He was extremely uncomfortable trying to determine where he could generate sales with a soon to be antiquated product. His only hope was to pivot to where the market provided the income.

In a similar way, a friend's son was murdered. He was a small business owner expanding his business, but with that trauma, he lost all desire to run his business beyond keeping the doors open. Understandably, he didn't want to pivot. Who wants to pivot to the

Next Normal when it requires burying a child? So, he went through the motions, marking time in that limbo segment of life. In time, he did pivot but reluctantly and cautiously.

Your challenge as a Pivotal Leader is to lead your team and organization into the best financial space. That challenge requires that you not only pivot but become pivotal, continually changing your perspective to see the best financial opportunities. The Next Normal isn't a plateau but rather a rugged mountain trail, rapidly and radically evolving. No wonder pivoting to the Next Normal financial space is often directly tied to pivoting into our Next Normal emotional space.

**Emotional Space**

Wherever you work, set your mind for work. This is your space, and when you are in that space, you are there to work. Be aware of the distractions, like the TV, phone, bills to pay, etc. Physically or emotionally removing those distractions works to focus, essentially silencing them.

That's the problem with the traditional office. You can't get what you need done because you are constantly interrupted by well-meaning and some not so well-meaning individuals. You can't concentrate and then become irritated or even angry with all the interruptions.

Limit your distractions. If you are working virtually, set those temptations aside until quitting time.

Don't answer the phone for personal calls. Leave the TV off. Don't be tempted to stream movies on your computer. Those are the easy items. Establishing boundaries has become more difficult during the pandemic as managers consider employment a 24/7 contract. This isn't healthy for the individual or the organization. Each of us needs a work-life balance to produce our best work.

Dr. Brian E Robinson writes in his book, *Chained to the Desk*, that workaholics tend to get less done because they a, take on too much work, b, don't delegate, and c, often end up being more disorganized than their coworkers. Patricia Thompson, Ph.D. notes that there are many health problems created by spending too much time at work. (HuffingtonPost.com)

To no one's surprise, stress not only kills but diminishes productivity.

One of the main culprits is electronic messaging. The solution is to set a time to check emails. Help establish the pattern with your manager, executive or team. Communicate to come to a shared meaning about this emotional distraction. Yes, communication is important, but you need time to focus. Work is like driving, don't be distracted. There are other ways to communicate urgent messages.

Individuals work best when they are valued and celebrated. Who wants to engage and create if they are taken for granted, dismissed, criticized, or ridiculed? Instead of engaging, they disengage. To foster that Next Normal emotional space, praise your team privately and publicly. Celebrate them where they feel as if you had just thrown them a lavish party. Preserve that energy by authentically valuing their contribution.

Some Old Normal leaders discount the value of emotional space, instead favoring the mechanical model of "crank it out" workers. Emotions are the spark that provides the innovation. Create a place where you are energized and where others feel that same empowerment.

Your challenge as a Pivotal Leader is to create a space where every team member is energized, engaged, and excited to help innovate the ultimate performance, production, and profits. That requires a safe and encouraging place to think.

**Intellectual Space**

We all need a place to think and create. It might be physical, but it is also emotional. There is a mindset we have when we enter that space. It might be an office or the shower. The important part is that we are free to think, create, and become.

Where is that intellectual space for you?

Unfortunately, many are not given that intellectual space. It might be because of the distractions or organizational rules. Imagine what "you aren't paid to think" does to a team member's desire to think. Now remember when a manager or executive too quickly dismissed your idea for solving a persistent problem. Notice how they essentially pushed you out of a physical space.

Each of us have a thinking room where we imagine, question, explore, challenge, reinforce, test, or expand our ideas. We all think but too many are not given the organizational space to develop our thinking. Pivotal Leaders recognize the value of each team member engaged intellectually to create the breakthrough innovation. All ideas are not equal but sometimes the smallest of ideas makes the biggest change. Remember what you read earlier, sometimes the craziest ideas lead to the breakthrough.

Intellectual activity must be grown like a farmer grows a crop. The ground must be prepared to receive the seed. After planting, the seed needs water and other nutrients as well as cultivating. Then it needs time to grow before harvesting. Throughout the process the plant needs a balance between tension and support. These tender plants grow into valuable employees when the Pivotal Leader times praise and pressure, support, and responsibility.

How can you provide that intellectual space for your team?

As a writer, I've found my intellectual space in my designated den at the back of the house. To foster that space emotionally, I've turned my desk away from the window so I'm not distracted and can focus on ideas. I need quiet while others need noise. I also need to know my ideas are important. To that end, I had to develop the habit of dismissing critics and focus on my audience. The hardest part was leaving the academic style of writing in favor of popular business books. Intellectually breaking that rule was intensely challenging.

Others choose to write in crowded coffee shops or writer retreats. They have their own intellectual challenges and rules to break.

Where is the best place for you to think?

Where is the best place for your team to think?

You might be surprised if you asked them.

Although I work at home and by myself, I need personal interaction to generate some of my best ideas. That is the same rule many have discovered from working remotely. They can "crank out" the daily, tactical assignments, but the intellectual stimulation is lacking, and innovations are impossible. Lacking is the needed resource, that spontaneous interaction technology companies have found so valuable. Innovators need friction caused by rubbing up against another's intellectual space to spark ideas. It doesn't happen in a vacuum.

How can you help create an intellectual space where the right friction is generated naturally?

## Career Space

Pivotal Leaders are naturally concerned with the viability of the organization. However, they recognize that change creates opportunities for every team member. We can't be selfish and short-sighted. As Zig Ziglar said, we will get what we want when we help others get what they want. The more we can help our team become successful in their careers, the more successful we will be.

That might be difficult for some Old Normal Leaders to accept. After all, the "grind it out" model also assumed a "grind them up" approach. Work members until they have nothing left to give and then get rid of them. That is opposite of the Pivotal Leader who values collaboration. The network of people willing to connect and create is the currency of the Next Normal. It's not hoarding but leveraging that power that leads to great innovations. That requires compassion, coming alongside another to help alleviate their pain. That is where the power comes from to energize a team. The team appreciates that you as the leader values their desires and dreams. Those that value stability, fear disruption. Those that value learning and growth, fear stagnancy. Understand their pain. Help alleviate their pain. Help those that desire development opportunities to grow.

In the end, two situations will develop. First, you will have many who will choose to stay with you. They will know, like, and trust you so much they won't want to leave. Second, you will develop a network of people and companies to solve your pain when you need it most. Together, you will find collaborators that will solve significant problems. Yes, it is a pay it forward model. Isn't that better than a "I wonder where I'll find the help I need it" model?

Your challenge is to find the Next Normal level of performance and production for each of your team members.

## Social and Recreational Space

We all need friends. Some need more than others but we all need that social contact with those we know, like and trust. We need a space where we can interact with fellow sports fans, outdoor enthusiasts, music lovers, or whatever hobby you enjoy. That's why bars and clubs are so important. People need a place to enjoy themselves with their friends.

Trauma shatters that space by taking away our desire to interact. We seclude ourselves when we are tending to our open wounds. While that is valuable for a time, sequestering ourselves for too long creates a warped perspective that squelches growth into the Next Normal. Imagine the connection you will make by helping someone reconnect after a personal trauma. Imagine how that will strengthen your team.

In the same way, employees who don't have anyone who they can connect with socially don't tend to stay long in a job. Imagine if we as Pivotal Leaders saw their pain and the pain it causes the organization in turnover. Now imagine how you can foster that social space with recreational activities, or at least, fostering a conversation about recreational activities.

REI, the Seattle outfitter, closes its retail stores on the day after Thanksgiving. Some might consider that foolish given it's one of the busiest shopping days of the year. However, they don't just close, but they also encourage their employees to lead the way and enjoy a day in nature. Imagine what that does to foster their business. It reinforces their product sales.

The challenge for Pivotal Leaders is to provide a Social and Recreational space that fosters relationships inside and outside the workplace. It's more than providing a basketball court or ping pong table. It is the emotional space where people can connect with what makes them happy.

**Family Space**

The industrial age took workers off the farm and out of the family-owned business into the factory and office. Where once people worked alongside their family members, progress separated families. Now the trend is reversing. Employees were sent home during the pandemic and required to compete with family members for a workspace. This has caused both serious family fractures and significant improvements. (frontiersin.org)

The message for Pivotal Leaders is that family is important. Family is critically important for many workers and the leader who recognizes that element of their lives will have the advantage. Decades ago, workers were told, "leave your problems at the door." That has changed to understanding that "those who are happy at home make the business better."

In that sense, compassionate leaders create a sense of family in the workplace. Again, Old Normal leaders will bristle at this. But look at the innovative teams. There is a sense of connection like the best of families. Those championship teams have a sense of camaraderie where players are there for each other.

What can you do to create that sense of family with your team?

Even though every family seems to have a dysfunction, and many are not close to their birth families, many drive a strong sense of belonging with their families. Many rank family at the top of their priorities. "Nothing comes before family."

To place work before family, especially in traumatic times, is counterproductive for Pivotal Leaders. Imagine what family members face when they lose a son yet are threatened with termination if they take a day off. Most bereavement leave is restricted to three days. In our world of living hours from our families, many times the loved one isn't even buried by the end of the three days. That doesn't begin to account for the emotional distress. Pivotal Leaders leverage that connection with family in an authentic, compassionate manner. Family is a powerful emotional connection. Foster it. Don't violate it.

At the same time, understand those with family disconnection. Providing a strong family connection at work may be the link to their ultimate pivot to the Next Normal.

Your challenge as a Pivotal Leader is overcome the family space obstacles in a way that that pivots everyone in the right direction and quickly into a much better situation.

**Ethical/Spiritual Space**

The final space Pivotal Leaders provide is the most delicate. Each of us abides by a set of ethics that is grounded in our spiritual values. That is not to be confused with a religious practice. I define spiritual as that connection to our energy that unleashes our ultimate. It is where we find strength to do what we never thought possible on our own. The spiritual fosters our dreams and fuels our passions. It is what makes our eyes light up, our ears perk up, and our smiles to beam. Our spiritual connection brings a bounce to our step and everyone notices.

Unfortunately, too many have not found their spiritual space. As I've written in several books, they haven't found their unique value, their prize inside. No wonder they challenge ethical guidelines and drain valuable emotional energy from the team with ego demands. Finding our unique value connects to what we find ultimately valuable in life. Once plugged into that source, nothing is impossible. That's why Pivotal Leaders need to be in tune with their team member's spirit. Celebrate their prize inside.

Unfortunately, many employees are frustrated because they are performing jobs that are not doing what they love. One report found that 53% were not happy at work. (Forbes.com) Imagine what that is doing to their performance, the departments production, and the company profits.

Now imagine how the trauma of personal disruption challenges their ethical and spiritual space. It could be a short- or long-term illness. It might be the strain of discord in the immediate or extended family. It could be any type of stress from work, community, or home. The disconnect spiritually might come from crossing a signature birthday that left them grieving their childhood or growing old. There are countless ways in which we all become spiritually disconnected.

This challenge may be the hardest challenge for the Pivotal Leader. Yet it may be the easiest and most productive. Your challenge is to overcome these spiritual challenges by celebrating that prize inside each team member. Find what makes them uniquely valuable. Praise them for it. Proclaim it to the rest of the team. In the end, that is why you want them on your team. If not, help them find the team to join where they will be celebrated.

**A Word of Wisdom**

Very few organizations will create a culture that overcomes these eight obstacles. That bar is extremely high but so is innovation and creating disruptive innovation. That doesn't mean becoming a Pivotal Leader is impossible.

There are many obstacles that Old Normal ignore. Your challenge isn't to be ordinary but rather to unleash the ultimate by thinking bigger, reaching higher, and doing what others dismissed as impossible. To do that, you must overcome significant obstacles with collaboration.

## Your Challenge

We have looked at these 8 areas previously in the book. My purpose in repeating them is to challenge you to think bigger about each one so you can reach higher. However, there are specific obstacles in each of these areas of our lives.

How can you provide more space for each of these areas in your world and your team's world?

# 18: COLLABORATE

Disruptive times demand that we shift paradigms because the old way of thinking no longer works like it used to. One of the paradigms that Tough Times, especially the COVID19 pandemic, is shattering is the competitive model. Major disruptions demand that we work together, collaborating to solve the significant problem.

The secret to crazy success in disruptive times is collaboration – not competition. That may ruffle the feathers of those Old Normal leaders.

**Pivotal Principle #18:**

**Collaboration vs Competition**

I've followed competitive sports my entire life. I love the way some teams surprise the experts and win against long odds. I also like to watch teams that sacrifice their ego to play together and make their game "sing like a finely tuned machine." Remember the Bobby Knight coached Indiana Hoosiers basketball team? They had a system of working together and their discipline was legendary.

Then there were other teams that relied on one or two superstar talents. Everybody knew who they were and enjoyed watching that level of talent on display.

If you are like me, you enjoy seeing the underdog knock off the favorite (unless our team is the favorite, right?) Remember the movie *Rocky, Cool Runnings* or *Seabiscuit*? Wasn't it fun to watch them fight through the odds to win?

Even though these were movies, they were based on real life underdog stories. Look farther and you find *The Miracle on Ice*, the story of the 1980 USA Men's Hockey Gold Medal win over the juggernaut Russian team. (I'm old enough to remember how that enthralled the nation.)

**The Vision**

How can a group of amateurs who had only won one gold (1960) and a few other Olympic medals defeat a team of professionals that had won 5 of the last 6 Gold Medals?

Obviously, they couldn't win on talent because the USA team was outmatched. They couldn't win because of their legacy because they didn't really have one. The Russian team had it all and were the heavy favorites.

But Herb Brooks, the USA coach, knew there was a way to topple this Goliath. It would take everyone buying into the vision. That required collaboration. Everyone had to believe, be conditioned and be relentless to win.

To do the impossible, they needed to believe they could deliver a miracle.

**Conditioning**

After a taxing conditioning period, they played a an exhibition schedule tougher than any USA hockey team had played before. As they say in sports, to be the best, you must beat the best. That requires physical and mental toughness.

Many quit when a coach pushes them too hard. That 1980 team was no exception. There were those who questioned Coach Brooks and his brutal program but eventually they bought into his vision and welcomed the challenge.

### Competition or Collaboration

To do what we never thought possible, we need collaborative teams that freely share ideas, energy, and vision. I'm sure the 1980 team would agree with Walt Disney that it is a lot of fun to do the impossible. It is exhilarating to do what we have never done before and solve persistent problems. But we cannot do that by ourselves. They knew they needed their teammates to beat the Russians and all the other competitors.

Typing the words doesn't create the climax but, as you already know, 1980 USA Hockey team brought everything they had and knocked off the Soviet Union. That win stunned the world and exhilarated the United States. Against all odds, they won.

But that didn't win the Gold. They still had to play the final game against Finland. That was no automatic win.

Each player had to give their all and play to the best of their ability. That is the same with any competition. However, collaboration has a team spirit. It is not just relying on the superstar but expecting that even the lessor player can make the critical difference. Collaboration is working together, freely giving whatever we have to offer, to make the team better and make the vision a reality.

### Playing for Each Other

Over the years I have talked with several championship athletes and watched even more interviewed on TV. I'm struck that almost all of them talk about how they played for their teammates. The same holds true for those members of the military going into battle. With their lives on the line, they freely gave everything for their buddies. Their buddies would do the same.

Sacrifice.

That is the key. Each team member sacrifices because they know everyone else will. They gladly collaborate to reach the vision.

**Collaboration**

Collaboration is working together, giving whatever is needed, to reach the seemingly impossible goal.

Unfortunately, too many don't understand how to collaborate. They promise but don't deliver and expect to get their rewards first. They are competitors, not collaborators, even though they are supposed to be on the same team. They don't freely sacrifice but compete for the best benefits. That is competition, not collaboration.

Competition does not yield the best results. Collaboration does. Ask Adam Grant. In his TED Talk on "Givers and Takers" he explains that the "Givers" make organizations the most successful. The "Takers" do give some benefit, but it only takes one "Taker" to ruin a good collaboration.

**Do You Believe in Miracles?**

The great sports announcer Al Michaels, in the final moments of the Gold Medal game, asked the provocative question, "Do you believe in miracles" as the underdog USA team finished the game.

I still remember watching the final game and cheering loudly. In the process, a life lesson was sinking into the back of my mind. "Do I believe in miracles?"

**Your Challenge**

## *PIVOTAL LEADERS*

Believing in the vision is critical to build a cutting-edge team and pivoting to the Next Normal. As a Pivotal Leader, your challenge is to find those individuals who will collaborate so you can both pivot and realize the opportunities in this next normal. When that happens, you can all break through to your ultimate level of success.

## 19: BREAK THROUGH

You can't be a writer unless you write. You can't be a performer until you perform. In the same way, you won't be a Pivotal Leader unless you pivot and seize your opportunity following the struggle. There is a time for dreaming and a time for discussion, planning, and questioning. There is time for strategy but without a breakthrough, it was little more than a wish. The challenge for Pivotal Leaders is to deliver the results.

To break through is to overcome the obstacles and reach the level of success you desire. It is to do what critics claimed couldn't be done, especially by you.

Pivotal Principle #19: Break Through

Imagine Edison quitting after the 500th failed experiment. Imagine the Apollo astronauts circling the moon but never landing. Imagine Martin Luther King shouting that he has a dream but never marching. Imagine the signers of the Declaration of Independence going home and saying, "That's enough. I'm satisfied.

Whatever your situation, ask yourself, "Will this crisis be your breakthrough moment?"

**Emma Gatewood**

Life hadn't been easy for Emma Gatewood. She was born to a family of 15 children and a father who suffered war injuries. Having lost his leg and no longer able to farm, he compensated with drinking and gambling. Life was difficult as she slept four to a bed, worked hard, and managed to complete eighth grade.

Along the way she developed a love for reading encyclopedias and strangely enough, the Greek classics. Living in the woods, she taught herself about wildlife and the plants nearby that could be used for medicine and food. It seems appropriate that she took up the hobby of writing poetry.

She must have thought, at age 19, she had broken through the difficult life when she met a primary school teacher, eight years older. Imagine how her love of learning led to fascinating discussions. They were soon married.

Her Next Normal would have been very promising. Life had to get better, right?

Unfortunately, that's where the story turned ugly. He husband left teaching and began farming tobacco. He worked her as hard as her father had. In addition to her household chores, she was required to burn tobacco beds, build fences, and mix cement. But that wasn't the worst part.

Her dreams were shattered when shortly after the marriage began, his mean streak emerged, and he started beating her. But it wasn't just her. He was convicted of manslaughter and sentenced to prison and restitution. Fortunately for him, the court showed mercy but only because he had nine children. He served no prison time. Back at home, he resumed the beatings of Emma, almost killing her several times. Her only sanctuary was running into the woods. After one brutal beating, he had her arrested and jailed. Yes, you read that correctly. He had her arrested. Finally, after she was given assistance by the mayor, she filed for divorce.

Why didn't she file divorce him earlier? Why didn't she seek refuse in a shelter? The answer is that it was 1940 and there were no shelters. Women rarely filed for divorce and if they did, they rarely won.

But Emma did. She had another chance and again pivoted to enter her Next Normal.

Fourteen years later, her love of learning revived, she happened onto an old copy of the August 1949 edition of *National Geographic* magazine. She was enthralled and intrigued with the article about the Appalachian Trail (A.T.). After everything she had been through, she had the crazy idea that she could hike the 2168 miles from Maine to Georgia. Never mind that she was 66 and this was 1954.

Like her marriage, the idea was enticing but didn't pan out. Even though the article promised that she needed "no special skill or training" she got lost, broke her glasses, and ran out of food just a few days into the venture. Rangers, as you can imagine in 1954, suggested this poor woman go home. She did.

But she didn't stay there, and she didn't give up her crazy dream. The following year, in 1955 and at the age of 67, she told her 9 children and 23 grandchildren that she was going out for a hike. She had no sleeping bag or tent, just a homemade denim bag with a shower curtain (to keep the rain off), a Swiss Army knife, a few other items. She wore her trusty Keds sneakers.

Along the way the press heard of her story and she became a bit of a celebrity, which brought some hospitality from locals. She not only slept along the trail, but also was offered a guest bed in private homes or a place on the porch to sleep. She even slept under a picnic table.

But the hike was no picnic. She found the trail challenging but wouldn't give up. After wearing out 7 pairs of Ked sneakers, she arrived at the south terminus of the trail in Georgia. In the process, she became the first woman to hike the A.T. in one season.

She repeated the unthinkable feat just two years later. Then, in 1959, at the age of 71, she hiked 2000 miles of the Oregon Trail, taking three months to travel on foot from St. Louis to Portland. In 1964, she became the first person to hike the A.T. when, at age 76, she hiked it in segments. By the end of her life, she had hiked more than 14,000 miles, equivalent to halfway around the world.

Even though her critics told her to stay at home and doubted she could hike the trail by herself, she said, "If men can do it, I can do it." (Wikipedia.com)

Notice Emma "Grandma" Gatewood broke through. She did it. Had she quit when her critics told her to go home in 1954, that's where the story would have ended. She could have quit dreaming when she was worked hard as a child. Why wasn't she a statistic after her dad turned to alcohol and gambling? Surely, she could have given up after almost dying at the hands of her husband. How embarrassed must she have been when her husband was convicted of manslaughter?

She didn't give up. She kept dreaming and pivoting into her Next Normal. She pushed through when life was extremely difficult. That is a strong message for all of us.

*There is no breakthrough without a breakdown.*
Tony Robbins

**Breakthrough via a Breakdown**

Tony Robbins recognizes that often our breakthrough moments come in a time of crisis. Something often needs to breakdown before we have the courage or intensity to push ourselves farther and higher. Might that been where Grandma Gatewood's found her resolve to do what many thought "impossible"?

But too often in the moment of crisis, we wilt. We give up just when our opportunity presents itself.

**Your Challenge**

Are you experiencing a Tough Time?
Are you giving yourself excuses?
Remember Grandma Gatewood.

Don't miss your opportunity to breakthrough. Use this breakdown to fuel your breakthrough with these three actions.
1. Change your paradigm.
2. See opportunities instead of obstacles.
3. Take the initiative to breakthrough your own barriers.

Difficult times give us cruel choices. Either we use those times to transform ourselves and our world or we let them get the best of us. It's one or the other. Tough Times are when the Tough get going and when others say, "It's too tough" and so they quit.

Which one are you?

Set your resolve to make this the time where you will break through.

## 20: THINK EVEN BIGGER

Pivotal Leaders enjoy the results of breaking though. Yes, Tough Times stink, but by thinking bigger and reaching higher, we find the results that we want. We recognize that Tough Times are a great opportunity to make that shift, creating or advancing our business, making more money, making a cultural difference. The key is to make that shift and enjoy the results.

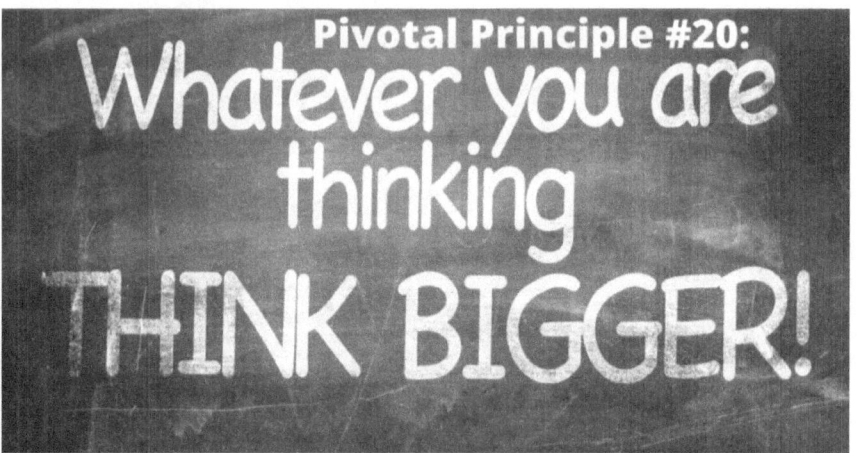

There are two critical points in that sentence. First, we achieve the results that we desired in the breakthrough. Second, we enjoy the results. Notice we can't enjoy the results if we do not achieve them.

In this post we examine five ways to enjoy the results of our breakthrough. Within these five, choose the results you want. Some want to make more money while others want to make a difference. This may seem contrary to many who are worried about just staying afloat. They claim they don't have time to do anything but put out the current fires. Remember Warren Buffet's investment strategy that the down-market is a great time to buy. That is when we find the best opportunities, but only if we have the right mindset. To succeed, we need to think bigger and reach higher.

## 1. Think Virtual.

This may be a no-brainer, for anyone who has come through the pandemic, but we must mention it. Use webinars, videoconferencing, or conference call lines to connect with current clients and attract new ones. Sales and marketing presentations may be even more effective using these methods, especially when most of us working from home. This is also a way to connect with current clients.

For those seeking a wider influence, going virtual is the way to change policies and help more people. The pandemic shutdown taught us that virtual might be the only way to reach those who are physically distanced. Going forward, almost everyone has a smart phone and checks it often. We have more of a need to connect and are looking for more ways to connect. There has never been a more appropriate time to utilize virtual that right now.

THINK BIGGER:

For your business needs, ask the following questions: How can you connect in new ways with current customers? What can you provide virtually that they want or need? How can you celebrate your relationships more?

## 2. Think Compassion

As my wife and I have written in *Leading with the Power of Compassion*, (soon to be retitled to *Engage Employees*) the most successful businesses come alongside their customers and employees to help alleviate their pain. You have been successful because you solved someone's problem, i.e., alleviated their pain. In Tough Times, our customers are in considerable pain. Instead of just thinking, "I can make more money," think, "I can make more money by solving more problems for my current customers." That is a big shift. Ask, "How can I help you today?"

That question is pivotal yet, so few ask it and fewer yet ask it authentically. Too many believe the real question is, "How can you help me?" They live in a self-centered world where they are consistently looking for others to solve their problems. I find that prevalent in not-for-profit organizations. What they don't understand is that there is much more energy generated from helping than begging. "Should" doesn't create a desire but a generous helping hand does.

For example, like many during the summer of 2020, my wife and I had to cancel several business and pleasure trips during the pandemic. We were pleasantly pleased when Alaska Airlines and American Airlines made cancellation painless. A single click or a simple phone call and our refunds we on the way. Painless!

Meanwhile we hear stories of other airlines making it much more difficult, claiming it would take approximately a year to receive a refund. Ouch!

On the other end of the spectrum, we had to file a home insurance claim. Even though they said they were there for us, they made it difficult at every step before denying the claim.

Then there is the Homeowners Association and their rules or the DMV. Why do they need to make things so difficult? Wouldn't it be far better for them to solve our problems instead of increasing the pain?

THINK BIGGER: What pain are your current customers feeling? How can you solve their problems with far less pain? How can you make their lives better?

### 3. Think New Markets

Tough Times force us to change. In that shift, we learn that old way no longer works as well as it once did. That forced change creates a pain for Old Normal Leaders. Meanwhile, the Pivotal Leaders find new markets for their current clients. They also create new products and services for their current clients.

Zoom increased their sales by 40% in 2020. (BBC.com)

Other tech companies have hurried into that new market. Even after the pandemic has waned, the need for virtual technology will persist.

As companied returned to the workplace following the pandemic shutdown, they realized their old pattern of in-person offices needed to be disrupted. Some opted to work completely virtual while others shifted to a hybrid model. Notice how that created a new market for any products or services. Imagine what that did for computers, and office equipment. I ordered a upgraded webcam but, like many others, couldn't get one for months. That's how much the market increased. Laptops were also in short supply.

Think back to World War II. Eleven percent of the male workforce joining the military. Meanwhile, manufacturing found new markets in building planes, tanks, and ammunition. Something had to give. Increased demand and reduced supply of workers. Employers found a new supply of workers by looking to the women who they had previously dismissed.

Now consider how you can help more hurting people. Black Lives Matters was created because of a persistent problem. They rallied in the summer of 2020 when George Floyd died in the hands of the police. That persistent prejudice was sparked in one tipping point incident in the same way that Candy Lightner created Mothers Against Drunk Driving decades earlier. Remember, our bruises can become our business, either for profit or not-for-profit. Sometimes we find new markets when there is attention drawn to a previously overlooked or too often dismissed problem. Following the pandemic, more attention should be given to the problems of isolation including drug usage, mental health, suicide, and elder care. With increased attention, those become new markets for both business and caring individuals.

THINK BIGGER: Think outside your current world to find new markets? Who now needs what you have been offering? How can you alleviate their pain better, faster, cheaper, or easier than those already in the market?

## 4. Think New Product Lines

Tough Times create pain for business leaders seeing their people and equipment sitting idle. Wise organizations think bigger and reach higher by exploring what other products or services they can supply.

For example, distilleries switched to making hand sanitizer. Sound crazy? How about car companies shifting production to make ventilator parts? In World War II, automobile manufactures switched to producing jeeps and tanks. These are great examples of modifying current equipment to make radically different products.

Think radically different. Hand sanitizer isn't just a new market for distilleries, it is a major shift. Use this opportunity to look beyond the work of your current market and product lines.

Apart from the pandemic, those going through traumatic times need a listening ear and a helping hand. How can you be the one who helps them make an exceedingly difficult pivot into the Next Normal?

As mentioned before, our misery can become our ministry. Our bruises can become our business. Whether you are looking to make more money or a bigger difference, this is the time to explore what products or services your market needs. They might need something that they didn't know was available. In that case, they need knowledge. They also might need products or services that they didn't before. That means there is an opportunity for you to create what they need or want.

THINK BIGGER: How can you use your current operations to provide desperately needed products? How can you shift temporarily? How can you shift permanently?

## 5. Think Radical Change

Change is often difficult. As humans, we love to live in what I call Civilization where life is predictable, safe, and comfortable. Why would anyone want to voluntarily change that if it is still working? Why would they want to leave that comfort zone?

Pivotal Leaders realize that the world is changing more rapidly and radically than ever before. The Next Normal will be disrupted by the Next Normal. What we thought was permanent often turns out to be temporary. The Pivotal Leader doesn't have the luxury to become comfortable and then being surprised by a disruption.

Instead, the Pivotal Leader must constantly consider radical change. It's not a matter of "if" the world will change radically, but "when" it will. They, i.e., we must become creators of change. We must become those who track the trends and forecast the opportunities. We can't afford to wait. We must shift our thinking now.

### Your Challenge

THINK BIGGER: Focus on change, radical change. What does your future look like when you correctly track the trends and forecast the opportunities? How much will your profits increase? How many people can you help?

Now consider what happens if you are content with being comfortable. What has surprised you in the past? What consequences did you suffer? Wouldn't you rather correctly anticipate the next disruption?

REACH HIGHER: What do you need to do to breakthrough to your next level of success?

# 21: MAKE DISRUPTION A HABIT

At 8:32 a.m. on May 18th, 1980, Mt. St. Helen's erupted. A lush landscape was almost instantly turned into a moonscape. But hidden in that anniversary of such radical disruption are 3 important lessons for those who aspire to be a disruptive leader.

Check out this video where the whole side of the mountain slid away followed by explosions. (Find the links in references of this book.) I grieve for those that lost their lives, but I am also appreciative what we can learn from this devastating natural occurrence.

**First, Be Willing to Change.**
Some, like the famous holdout Harry Truman, refused to leave his lodge and suffered his demise. Like Harry, we can be obstinate to change, dig in our heels and sit on our comfortable front porch where, unfortunately, we will be obliterated by the blast of sudden change. We all have a decision to make. Leaders watch the trends and choose to prepare so they are not a casualty of rapid and radical change.

**Second, Be Wise in Taking the Risk**
Many thought they were safe that Sunday morning because they stayed outside the government's restricted zone. Unfortunately, the government didn't get it right and the blast was far worse than predicted and 57 people lost their lives. The lesson we can take from

that tragedy is that disruption is difficult to predict. No one really knows the exact moment it will occur. The sad part is that most of those who died did not need to be there. They were hiking, camping, and fishing - not working. Was it really that important to be that close? No. The recreation could have waited, or they could have gone somewhere else.

**Third, Prepare for the Recovery**

The eruption of Mt. St. Helen's destroyed a pristine landscape, and many wondered if it would ever recover. But it wasn't long and green shoots began to push through the layers of ash and not long later the animals returned. Today, there are still signs of disruption, but the landscape has recovered quite well.

That is a lesson for leaders today. Many give up hope when such drastic disruption occurs. They quit looking ahead, instead focus solely on what was lost. They miss an important lesson: What appears to be permanently devastated will soon become manageable and filled with great opportunities. If continue to look ahead and prepare for dramatic change, we can sense and seize the best opportunities before anyone else.

Most won't understand a leader's desire to disrupt a comfortable situation. Followers enjoy comfort because that is what they work for. But not leaders. We love disruption. We love the challenge and the competition. We love the sense of creating and becoming, of cashing in on being first and making the significant difference. We also hate following and know that getting too comfortable is a critical error, one that usually turns a leader into a follower. Being too comfortable simply isn't smart, logical or strategic so those of us who are committed to leading don't get too comfortable.

Don't get me wrong, we all like a little comfort. We like to enjoy a win and take the edge off just a bit. We get that. But when we get so comfortable that we are no longer compelled to staying on the cutting edge, that is when the problems start and too soon, we are falling behind. It usually happens when we extend a moment of success into a slumber that feels so good but leaves us lazy, lethargic, and left behind. No leader wants that. But it gets worse. When we relax too much and then fall behind, we tend to PANIC when we do wake up. In that panic we react rather than plan, we let emotion override logic and problems become a leader's nightmare. We don't want that.

So, what do we do? The job of a leader is to constantly look ahead,

anticipate problems and solve them beforehand. Here are five compelling reasons to stay on that cutting edge, developing a habit of disruption even when we would like to relax and be a little more comfortable.

**1. Change is Constant - Stability is Temporary**

Once we reach a certain level of success, often we wrongly assume that the good times will last. But we know that is not the case. If we are not in a mindset of constant change, we will likely let up, relax, and slow down. That is when the problems start. Stay on cutting edge, make change the constant.

**2. We Cannot Stop Natural Attrition**

Things are constantly ending and need to be replaced. That is simply a law of nature. Clients leave for a variety of reasons and if we get too comfortable, we quickly see our progress slowing as well. Change happens consistently. We might as well get used to living with this law of nature.

**3. Comfortable Quickly Becomes Complacency**

When we are hungry, we tend to work harder. But when we have a little success and things are a little easier, we like to reward ourselves and relax a bit. That is the critical point. Unless we keep that consistent drive alive, we can become content to sit back and live with the limited success we just achieved. Don't become complacent with the status quo.

**4. Comfortable Changes our Focus**

Disruptive leaders are actively looking to do what has never been done before, at least in their own industry, community, or business. But with even a little comfort, we change our focus from disrupting to maintaining. We cease playing offense and decide to defend, no longer playing to win but simply trying not to lose. That usually doesn't turn out too well. Always play to win.

**5. First Choice is Best**

Let's be honest, the first to sense and seize an opportunity usually enjoys a big advantage. You must love that because it is better than leftovers. As leaders, we live for the best opportunities so why would we ever want to start at a disadvantage? Set your strategy to be the first to disrupt.

**YOUR CHALLENGE**

Building habits makes innovation a regular occurrence instead of wishful thinking or a happy accident.

Welcome innovative thinking.

Welcome respectful thinking that differs from yours.

Challenge your team to find innovative solutions to persistent problems.

Reconsider ideas and solutions you have dismissed in the past.

# YOUR PIVOTAL CHALLENGE

Having finished reading this book, envision yourself five years from today. Imagine that how you immediately implemented three of the 21 principles. Now imagine how implementing those three principles have changed your life. List the improvements. How has it helped you in your career? How has it helped financially? How has it helped your leadership?

Choose one word that describes how you feel five years from today?

Now again imagine that scene five years from today. Only this time, you are reminded that you got distracted and never implemented even one of the concepts. Imagine how frustrating it will be to suffer with some of the same problems as you have now. Imagine the regret that you will have knowing it could have been different. Imagine what it feels like to know you could have made the difference but didn't.

I challenge you to adopt just one of these principles. Commit to focusing on that principle for the entire week. Start the morning thinking about it. Reread the chapter or a paragraph. Write down how you want to implement it. Remind yourself of how you want to change your leadership, career, and or life.

I've taken the time to write this book to help you pivot through the challenges to see the best opportunities. If I have helped you make one small step, it has been worth my time. Imagine what it will be worth to you.

Caution: Just reading the book and adding knowledge may be enjoyable but rarely makes the significant change. Instead, deliberate action toward a specific goal paves the path of success. I offer a free 20-minute consultation/coaching call for those interested. No hard sell, I promise.

*Loren Murfield, Ph.D.*
Loren@MurfieldCoaching.com

# PIVOTAL LEADER CHECKLIST

- [ ] 1. TRACK THE TRENDS
- [ ] 2: STAY FOCUSED
- [ ] 3: ENGAGE YOUR TEAM
- [ ] 4: FOSTER AN INNOVATIVE CULTURE
- [ ] 5: FIND YOUR UNIQUE VALUE
- [ ] 6: CHALLENGE YOUR TEAM
- [ ] 7: COMMUNICATE
- [ ] 8: SHARE YOUR INNOVATIVE VISION
- [ ] 9: LEVERAGE FEAR
- [ ] 10: LEVERAGE PAIN
- [ ] 11: BE AGGRESSIVE IN YOUR STRATEGY
- [ ] 12: FOSTER DISRUPTION
- [ ] 13: RETHINK REJECTION & FAILURE
- [ ] 14: CREATE A CUTTING-EDGE ATTITUDE
- [ ] 15: FOSTER FLEXIBILITY
- [ ] 16: BREAK THE RULES
- [ ] 17: OVERCOME ANY OBSTACLES
- [ ] 18: COLLABORATE
- [ ] 19: BREAK THROUGH
- [ ] 20: THINK EVEN BIGGER
- [ ] 21: MAKE DISRUPTION A HABIT

# REFERENCES

"Amazon Warehouse Robots," Mind Blowing Videos on YouTube.com
https://www.youtube.com/watch?v=cLVCGEmkJs0

Anirudh, "10 Most Famous Graffiti Artists in the World." In Learnodo-Newtonic.com (October 7, 2017)

Banksy.com (original August 7, 2014, updated June 15, 2020).
https://www.biography.com/artist/banksy
https://www.learnodo-newtonic.com/famous-graffiti-artists

Bariso, J. "In 1 Powerful Sentence, Mark Cuban Just Gave Every Company in America a Harsh Wake-up Call." Inc. (July 29, 2019)

Burkard, C. "The Joy of Surfing In Ice-Cold Water" Ted.com. (June 3, 2015)

Burris, D. "Flash Foresight." Harper Collins Publishers. (2011)

Cancialosi, C. (2017, July 17) What is Organizational Culture? Retrieved from https://gothamculture.com

"Caregiver Statistics: Demographics," in Caregiver.org.
https://www.caregiver.org/caregiver-statistics-demographics

"Coronavirus: New test results find 31 positive cases at Life Care Center in Kirkland," Associated Press in Q13 Fox News. (March 9, 2020)
https://q13fox.com/2020/03/09/coronavirus-new-test-results-find-31-positive-cases-at-life-care-center-in-kirkland/

Courtney, E. "The Benefits of Working From Home: Why The Pandemic Isn't the Only Reason to Work Remotely" Flexjobs.com
https://www.flexjobs.com/blog/post/benefits-of-remote-work/

"Doctor dragged off United Airlines flight says he 'cried' watching the video"
YouTube.com Apr 9, 2019
https://www.youtube.com/watch?v=_anhvdWf3DM

Gallup, State of the American Workplace (2017). Gallup.com.

Evans, S., Mikocka-Walus, A., Klas, A., Olive, L., Sciberras, E., Karantzas, G., Westrupp, E. "From "It Has Stopped Our Lives" to "Spending More Time Together Has Strengthened

Bonds": The Varied Experiences of Australian Families During COVID-19" in Frontiers in Psychology (October 20, 2020). https://www.frontiersin.org/articles/10.3389/fpsyg.2020.588667/full

"Grandma Gatewood" Wikipedia.com https://en.wikipedia.org/wiki/Grandma_Gatewood

Grandview Research: "Chatbot Market Size, Share & Trends Analysis Report By End User, By Application (Bots For Service, Bots For Marketing), By Type (Standalone, Web-based), By Product Landscape, By Vertical, And Segment Forecasts, 2021 – 2028. https://www.grandviewresearch.com/industry-analysis/chatbot-market?mod=article_inline

Granger, J. "Sobering Statistics about Readers" (October 20, 2019) https://www.hogwartsprofessor.com/sobering-statistics-about-readers-today/

Grant, A. "Are you a giver or a taker?" TED.com (November, 2016) https://www.ted.com/talks/adam_grant_are_you_a_giver_or_a_taker

"Higher wage workers more likely than lower wage workers to have paid leave benefits in 2018," TED: the Economics Daily in U.S.

Bureau of Labor Statistics (August 3, 2018) https://www.bls.gov/opub/ted/2018/higher-wage-workers-more-likely-than-lower-wage-workers-to-have-paid-leave-benefits-in-2018.htm

Ibarra, H, and Hansen, M.T., Harvard Business Review. (July–August 2011) https://hbr.org/2011/07/are-you-a-collaborative-leader

James, G. "Who turned tragedy into success." Inc. magazine (July 20, 2012) https://www.inc.com/geoffrey-james/3-who-turned-tragedy-into-success.html

Jiang, J. "What I learned from 100 days of rejection" TED.com (December 7, 2016)

Kim, W., Mauborgne, R. *Blue Oceans Strategy* (2005) Harvard Business School Press.

Kipman, S. "15 Highly Successful People Who Failed On Their Way To Success" Lifehacks.com (March 20, 2021) (https://www.lifehack.org/articles/productivity/15-highly-successful-people-who-failed-their-way-success.html)

Levitin, D. J. *Successful Aging* (2020: Dutton.)

Lister, K. "Work-At-Home After Covid-19—Our Forecast." Global Workplace Analytics. https://globalworkplaceanalytics.com/work-at-home-after-covid-19-our-forecast

Lukianoff, G., Haidt, J. "The codling of the American Mind." Penguin Books, (2018)

Leprince-Ringuet D. "Technology will create millions of jobs." Zdnet.com. (March 19, 2021) https://www.zdnet.com/article/technology-will-create-millions-of-jobs-the-problem-will-be-to-find-workers-to-fill-them/

Lister, K. "Latest Work-At-Home/Telecommuting/Mobile Work/Remote Work Statistics" (June 20, 2021) https://globalworkplaceanalytics.com/telecommuting-statistics

Mahlum, A. "There's No Way This Will Work" TED Talk on YouTube. (October 5, 2013). https://www.youtube.com/watch?v=q2lhrGgwdSI

Mt. St. Helens Videos, USGS. (May 18, 1980) https://www.usgs.gov/observatories/cascades-volcano-observatory/mount-st-helens-videos

Munster, G. "Here's When Having a Self-Driving Car Will Be a Normal Thing," (September 13, 2017) Fortune Magazine. http://fortune.com/2017/09/13/gm-cruise-self-driving-driverless-autonomous-cars/

National Institute of Health: Suicide Statistics. https://www.nimh.nih.gov/health/statistics/suicide

Needle David. Business in Context: An Introduction to Business and Its Environment, 2004. ISBN 978- 1861529923. Needle David. Business in Context: An Introduction to Business and Its Environment, 2004. ISBN 978-1861529923.

Pelley, S. "Facial and emotional recognition; how one man is advancing artificial intelligence" 60 Minutes, CBS News, (Jan 13, 2019)

https://www.cbsnews.com/news/60-minutes-ai-facial-and-emotional-recognition-how-one-man-is-advancing-artificial-intelligence/

Perrin, A. "Who doesn't read books in America?" (September 26, 2019)
https://www.pewresearch.org/fact-tank/2019/09/26/who-doesnt-read-books-in-america

Pinak, P. "Ronnie Lott Chopped His Pinky Off So He Didn't Miss a Game" In FanBuzz,com, (June 17, 2021)
https://fanbuzz.com/nfl/ronnie-lott-pinky/#:~:text=The%20former%20San%20Francisco%2049ers,after%20a%2010%2D6%20record.

Prochaska, J., DiClemente, C., Norcross, J. "In Search of How People Change" American Psychological Association, Vol. 47., #9, (September, 1992.

PwC.com
2018 AI Predictions. "Employer Impact"
https://www.pwc.com/us/en/services/consulting/library/artificial-intelligence-predictions/employer-impact.html
"How education will impact jobs"
https://www.pwc.co.uk/services/economics/insights/the-impact-of-automation-on-jobs.html

Robinson, B. *Chained to the Desk* 3rd Ed. (2014). NYU Press.

Semuels, A. ALANA "Millions of Americans Have Lost Jobs in the Pandemic—And Robots and AI Are Replacing Them Faster Than Ever." Time. (August 6, 2020).
(https://time.com/5876604/machines-jobs-coronavirus/)

Sturt, D. and Nordstrom, T. "10 Shocking Workplace Stats You Need To Know" in Forbes.com (March 8, 2008) (https://www.forbes.com/sites/davidsturt/2018/03/08/10-shocking-workplace-stats-you-need-to-know/?sh=5ae8fcff3afe)

Thompson, P. "Workaholism Doesn't Make You More Productive. Here's Why." HuffPost, (May 25, 2017) https://www.huffpost.com/entry/workaholism-doesnt-make-you-more-productive-heres_b_58dc032fe4b07f61a2bb8add

U.S. Bureau of Labor Statistics
https://www.bls.gov/opub/ted/2018/higher-wage-workers-more-likely-than-lower-wage-workers-to-have-paid-leave-benefits-in-2018.htm

"Witness the volcanic eruption of Mount Saint Helens and subsequent flooding wrought by melted glaciers," Briticannia.com (May 18, 1980)
https://www.britannica.com/video/82384/awe-geologists-explosion-Mount-Saint-Helens-May-18-1980

"Zoom sees more growth after 'unprecedented' 2020" BBC.com (March 1, 2021)
https://www.bbc.com/news/business-56247489

*PIVOTAL LEADERS*

# PIVOTAL LIVING AND WORKING SERIES

Available at www.PivotalLiving.org and www.BetterYou.TV and Amazon.com

*PIVOTAL LEADERS*

# GUIDED BUSINESS MEDITATIONS from the NATIONAL PARKS SERIES

# GUIDED MEDITATIONS from the NATIONAL PARKS SERIES

Available at www.PivotalLiving.org and www.BetterYou.TV and Amazon.com

*PIVOTAL LEADERS*

# VIDEO COURSES and SERIES

Fundamentals for Your Success
        Building Your Competence
        Building Your Reputation
        Building Your Confidence
        Building Your Skills
        Building Your Leadership
Pivotal Listening: Building Better Skills to Create Your Personal and
        Business and Breakthrough
5 Steps to Find Your Unique Value
Doc's Daily Video Series
        Resurrection Sunday
        Motivational Monday
        Think Bigger Tuesday
        Why Not Reach Higher Wednesday
        Try Running Thursday
        Friday Meditations from the National Parks
        Strategic Saturday
Living 100% A.L.I.V.E.

*www.BetterYou.TV*

*PIVOTAL LEADERS*

## NOW AVAILABLE

## ABOUT THE AUTHOR

Dr. Loren Murfield is an innovative thinker who serves as an Executive Coach, Author, and Speaker. He holds a Ph.D. in Communication Studies from the University of Nebraska and authored nearly 50 books and multiple online and in-person courses. His books address business, professional, and personal development. Working with entrepreneurs and organizational leaders, he stretches their thinking to see cutting-edge opportunities.

He has also written and acted in a movie short, wrote, staged, and acted in eight plays. In 2022-23, he ran 6 marathons in the year he turned 68.

Life is indeed too short to settle for the ordinary limitations others place upon us.

Website: www.PivotalLiving.com
Email: Loren@MurfieldCoaching.com

www.ingramcontent.com/pod-product-compliance
Lightning Source LLC
Chambersburg PA
CBHW031621210526
45464CB00004B/1686